FROM CRADLE TO COLLEGE

(And Everything in Between)

Author of *New York Times* bestseller
Money Doesn't Grow on Trees

FROM CRADLE TO COLLEGE *(And Everything in*  *Between)*

A PARENT'S GUIDE TO FINANCING YOUR CHILD'S LIFE

Neale S. Godfrey WITH TAD RICHARDS

HarperBusiness
A Division of HarperCollins*Publishers*

HarperCollins books may be purchased for educational, business, or sales promotional use. For information please write: Special Markets Department, HarperCollins Publishers, Inc., 10 East 53rd Street, New York, NY 10022.

FIRST EDITION

Designed by Irving Perkins Associates

Library of Congress Cataloging-in-Publication Data

Godfrey, Neale S.
    From cradle to college (and everything in between) : a parent's guide
to financing your child's life / Neale Godfrey with Tad Richards.
    — 1st ed.
        p.   cm.
    ISBN 0-88730-723-X
    1. Parents—Finance, Personal.   2. Finance, Personal.
I. Richards, Tad.   II. Title.
HG179.G628   1996
332.024′0431— dc20   95-37151

96 97 98 99 00 ❖/RRD 10 9 8 7 6 5 4 3 2 1

This book is dedicated with equal parts love and respect to Dr. Irving Dardik and Alison Godfrey-Dardik, two people who have taught me more about courage, wisdom, and grace than I ever believed was possible.

In every time there are voices of truth, eyes of vision, souls of pioneering spirit of pure scientific inquiry; and sadly, in every time, there are small minds who would stifle that vision for selfish reasons.

Always, ultimately, it is the courage and truth we honor. Irv and Alison, there are those who honor your courage and truth even in the time of your darkest tribulation. And you will prevail.

With love,
Neale

⚜ Contents

❧ Acknowledgments

First, we'd like to thank Cindy Bell, our researcher for this book, who found everything we needed from her and anticipated things we didn't know we needed yet.

Don Bell was instrumental in helping develop the time-line concept.

Thanks to Laurie Della Villa-Miller and Pat Richards, to Bob, Jeannie, Heather, and Puma Richards of EPA Financial Services, Inc., Toms River, N.J. Thanks to Suzanne Oaks, Lisa Berkowitz, and Adrian Zackheim. Thanks to Peter Ginsberg and Eric Martins. Thanks to Sue and Dan.

❧ Introduction

Would you hop into your car today, drive down to your local discount store, and buy a new TV set for $334 without stopping for a moment to see where it fits into your budget?

Probably not. OK, then . . . would you decide to remodel your kitchen, and dash off a check to a contractor for $3,340 without taking some time to see where it fits into your budget and whether your cash flow situation can accommodate it?

Not likely.

OK, try this one: Would you go down to your local car dealership and plunk down $33,400 for a new luxury car without seriously going over your budget to figure out how you're going to finance it and what other purchases you'll have to forgo in order to make this one?

Say, shouldn't these questions be getting harder? Obviously, you're not going to spend like this. No way. No time.

OK, one more question: Would you commit to a purchase of $334,000 without developing a serious, long-term budgetary strategy to figure out where the money's going to come from, and how you're going to work it into your overall budget?

Of course you wouldn't.

Would you?

Well, most of us do.

That $334,000 is what the Family Economics Research Group (FERG) of the United States Department of Agriculture has calculated as the cost of basic household expenditures, from birth to age 17, for a child born in 1993.

That's a basic figure. It's FERG's calculation for one child, born into a two-parent family, in the highest overall income group (defined as an annual income of more than $54,400 for the entire family), but it's also a bare-bones figure. (The tables in the appendix give a more detailed breakdown of this and other totals, with explanations of the figures and how they were arrived at.)

From Cradle to College is a tool for calculating that $334,000—or whatever your actual figure climbs to—and integrating it into your budget. More than that, this book is a tool for planning, for coping, for developing a strategy to facilitate the financial part of raising a child. It is aimed at parents—and people who plan to be parents—who are looking at the future and wondering: How are we going to manage?

This isn't a question that goes away as your children get older, either, so the yardsticks and techniques here should be useful for the parents of older children as well. We always need to figure out how we're going to manage, and there are always solutions. They won't be as complete if your oldest is 16 and you're just starting to think about college, but there are always better ways to manage your money, so I'll be talking to parents—and grandparents—in every age bracket.

Children are money-eating machines. Everything that you expect them to do costs money. Everything that you don't expect them to do, they'll do also, and that will cost money, too. You know this to be true, and as a result, there is no part of your financial life that needs to be planned more carefully.

Kids don't change much. Their needs—food, shelter, clothing, education—are constant. Their wants—what the other kids have, whatever's bad for them—may be unpredictable, but it is predictable that every kid will have some of them. Their dreams and aspirations—bold and exciting, and sometimes breathtaking—cost money to realize. Your needs—quality time with them, a little time away from them—are a guarantee.

What does change is the world you bring those children into. As the twentieth century winds down, financial opportunities are shrinking, and costs—particularly the cost of education—are skyrocketing. How much? Well, if a child is born today and if she graduates from Harvard in the class of 2017 and pays full tuition—and if tuition costs keep rising at the rate they're going—it will cost another $66,000 for four years and a bachelor's degree.

Things are tougher today. Money is tighter, options are narrower, and the big expenses—a house, college—are huge. To give your children the same kind of start in life that your generation got from its parents means that you have to understand this entire new financial terrain.

This is the first comprehensive guide to the biggest, most important, most complicated financial arrangement you will ever have: financing the lives of your children. Like no other book before it, this volume will help you consider a wide range of financial arrangements that you'll need to enter into, or develop, or reevaluate from before the birth of your child through every phase of his/her development through your own old age and even after your death.

Having kids is the one permanent, irrevocable decision you'll make in life. Jobs, homes, hometowns, even marriages can be left behind, but your children are always a part of you. And they're also your most important financial decision—they will be the major expenditure for the rest of your life, and will influence every financial decision you make for the rest of your life.

A Comprehensive Financial Strategy

Many books take up the subject of being financially prepared for your child's future, but too many of them concentrate on one thing: paying for college.

Well, it's true—education is important. But it's only part of the story of financing your child's life. Too often, however, it's the only part of the story that people consider, or the only part that they're encouraged to consider.

There was a time when a financial strategy for your child's future meant just that: paying for college. Now it means everything. There is no area of your life—the part of your life that requires financial planning—that is not affected by your children.

Think about this. Actually, there are two ways to think about it. The first is: Having a baby is going to let me in for all that? Which way is the nearest convent?

The second, once you've sat down, fanned yourself gently, done a few deep breathing exercises, and thought through it again, is: These are pretty much all the details of life that I'd have to work out anyway.

It's not as though if you didn't have children, you wouldn't have to do anything about petty stuff like work and shelter. But when you do have children, or when you're starting to plan for children, those kids will play a crucial part in all these decisions, and you're a whole lot better off if you understand just what that part is.

I'm not suggesting that the decision to have children should be a financial one, and I'm certainly not going to set any financial guidelines for deciding to become a parent. But once you've made that first decision to begin thinking about a family, you should be aware of all the financial ramifications of that decision.

This is the first book to examine, across the board, all the financial decisions that stem from being a parent, and it is the first to focus specifically on how these decisions affect your whole financial future, and your child's financial future. With extensive cross-referencing for easy access to information, I'll organize these issues both by stages of life, yours and your child's (from the child's birth and infancy through college and independence, and on through your own old age and death) and by issues (health care and insurance, college, day care for preschoolers, etc.). I'll outline patterns for the gradual transfer of responsibility and decision making from parent to child, and this will be one of the most important areas of emphasis in our book, and one that sets it apart from other financial guides.

This is also the first book of its kind to deal with the realities of today's America—a time and place in which traditional rules don't apply. The expectation that your job would be over when you saw your kids through college may no longer apply—24 percent of grown children come home to live with their parents at some time after they move out, frequently bringing children of their own with them. You can't count on your major financial events to follow a predictable pattern— with people having children later, with people living longer, you could easily find your kids' college years, your own plans for retirement, and your parents' need for extensive nursing and medical care all ganging up on you at the same time. And those major financial events are getting even larger—it's not out of line to estimate that 25 percent of your income will go to your kids' college education—at a time when planning seems to have gone out of style. Americans have the lowest savings rate in the industrialized world.

Within each chapter, I will give you advice on how to approach the particular issue at different ages and stages (this means stages of both your kids' lives and your own). The earlier you begin, the better you can make things, but there's always something you can do. I'll give you ideas on how to reevaluate your decisions as time goes on. Sometimes you'll just be doing regular maintenance, but sometimes you'll need to do a major reevaluation for extraordinary circumstances— the addition of more children to the family, a sudden change of financial circumstances (for good or bad), illness or accident, or the recognition of a particular talent or interest.

In no case will I presume to advise you on how to raise your children. Instead, I'll be focusing on how to weigh financing alternatives intelligently, and determine the "opportunity costs" involved (weighing alternatives in terms of the relative returns on alternate financial strategies—for example, is it more cost-effective in the long run to send your children to public or private school?) and the "time value of money" (pay now, or pay later—for example, the cost of prenatal care *vs.* later costs if this investment is not made). These are daunting financial terms, but they are not hard to understand and are absolutely relevant to your home budgeting and your daily life. I'll show you how you can not only save money but maximize your return on investments—including some surprising alternatives that may help you achieve your goals. I'll give you objective ways to help you quantify the costs of some of those goals. I'll tell you how to use yardsticks—you have to know how to figure out these costs for all circumstances, because tax codes change and the economy changes.

My approach is to:

Give you parameters to use in setting goals for you and your kids.

Give you enough flexibility to allow for goal shifting and changes in financial circumstance (including disaster).

Help you identify priorities within goals.

Help you identify needs and wants.

Delineate between fixed costs and variable costs.

Explain the concepts and show you how to figure opportunity costs, return on investment, and time value of money in terms of goals for your kids.

Give you references for further information.

Show you how all this is doable by demystifying the process.

Of course, it won't be as dry as all that. I couldn't do that if I tried. I only spend part of my time in the financial world. The rest of the time I use the language you learn when kids track mud into the kitchen or hold up their arms to hug you at bedtime. The situations I'm describing in this book I've either lived through or have friends who've lived through them.

So I'll talk about what it feels like, first—the human situation. Next, the nuts and bolts: I'll take you through setting up a wish list, a series of priorities: Do you want a life insurance policy that will take care of your children for life, or just see them through college? Do you want your baby to go to Harvard some day, or a state college? Has a big wedding always been an important tradition in your family, or a bar/bas mitzvah, or a Sweet Sixteen, or cosmetic surgery?

Then I'll present a complete array of financial alternatives and options, and worksheets so you can tailor the options to your goals, focus on fixed and variable costs (relating to needs and wants), figure out what slice of the whole pie your desired options will take, and if necessary rearrange your priorities (in fact, these priorities should be reevaluated regularly).

Keep in mind—the above wish list may sound as though it's moving in descending order of importance, from the serious (life insurance) to the frivolous (cosmetic surgery), but this is not the case, and I will certainly not be treating it as such. I'll be explaining the difference between fixed and variable costs, but I'll also emphasize that all these decisions involve an outlay of money, the quality of your own and your child's life, and key steps in the all-important continuum of the transfer of financial responsibility from you to your child.

Finally, I'll list the best reference materials on each subject.

All of this is aimed at a single goal: creating and implementing a master plan that will ensure that your kids get the best you can give them . . . and make sure you survive the process.

Are your kids worth it all? If you're like most parents, sometimes you'll wonder. But what you know instinctively is the absolute truth: Your children are the best investment you'll ever make, and they deserve, at the very least, the same care and planning you put into the rest of your financial life.

Sue and Dan

To demonstrate how these decisions can work in real life, I've created a fictional couple, Sue and Dan. They're based on people I know, and people I've counseled, but I decided to create a fictional family because I can give them alternate lives. No, not alternate lifestyles—Sue and Dan are solid, industrious, middle-class Americans. I'm talking about *real* alternate lives: This is Sue and Dan when their plans materialize; this is Sue and Dan when those same plans don't work out and they have to create new strategies.

We'll be following Sue and Dan through the course of this book. I hesitate to say that their lives are typical (nobody's lives are typical), but their problems are typical: How to provide the best for their children and the *strategy* of their problem solving—not necessarily the solutions themselves—represent what I feel to be an intelligent, well-prepared way of going about it.

Sue and Dan, when we first meet them, are newlyweds, planning their future. She's 27; he's 25; they're both college graduates; Sue has an MBA. They live in New York City. Sue is an investment banker with a large financial institution, comfortable within the corporate structure. She makes $65,000 a year and can count on a bonus of $20,000 to $30,000. Dan is an electrical contractor, working for a large contracting firm. He makes $35,000 a year now, but has his sights set on starting his own business.

They both want a family: two children, the first one as soon as possible, the second one three years later.

We'll follow Sue and Dan as they prepare for the financial milestones in their lives, and the lives of their children.

Dream Lists

The next thing they'll do is to start making their dream list.

You might as well start with your dreams. It's your chance to imagine everything you could possibly want for your child . . . balanced with a little dose of reality. I've put this in terms of need *vs.* want . . . those things you *know* you're going to have to find money for, and those things you hope you'll be able to manage.

Your Dream List

DREAM	HIGH PRIORITY	IF THINGS WORK OUT
EDUCATION		
Private preschool		
Private elementary school		
Private high school		
College		
ENRICHMENT — COURSES, CLASSES		
Art		
Music, dance		
Sports		
Languages		
Computer skills		
Summer camp		

(continued on next page)

DREAM	HIGH PRIORITY	IF THINGS WORK OUT
CHILD CARE		
Live-in nanny		
Regular day-care		
TRAVEL		
Summer vacation trips		
Disney World		
Foreign travel		
FOR THE PARENTS—TIME ALONE		

(continued on next page)

Dream	High Priority	If Things Work Out
Things to Buy		

These are just a few suggestions to start you thinking. I've left plenty of room for you to add on to it; your dreams are your own. Just check the appropriate box, or put your initial in it to distinguish between your dream list and your partner's.

The guidelines are simple. Is it a high-priority item for you? Or is it something you'd like if you have some extra savings, but not something you'd spend money on first? If it's something you're not interested in at all, just leave both boxes blank. Then check over your responses. There's no exact formula here, but if you have a heavy preponderance of "High Priorities," you may find you're going to have to rethink a few of them. If you don't have enough "High Priorities," you may be setting your sights too low.

Sue and Dan, who are planning to have two children and two careers, would like to have a live-in nanny (which will also affect the size of their dream house). They are thinking of sending their children to a private Montessori school for the early grades, then to public school for junior high and high school.

They want to send their kids to camp and make it possible for them to have private lessons year-round in areas that interest them. Dan, who played guitar in high school and college, marks "Music lessons"—after all, it's his dream list, but he knows the kids will ultimately decide for themselves. "Still," he says, "two years of piano lessons anyway, so they'll have a good, solid understanding of music." They know that no one knows what the technology of the future will be, but subject to change, they plan for one family computer and one for Sue's business.

They plan on having three cars—one for each of them, for primary use, and one for the nanny (and, in later years, for the kids).

They'd like to eat out—alone—two or three times a week, to get away from the house and talk to each other in a relaxed setting.

Sue puts a high priority on clothes and dressing well; Dan is less interested in this, but they both agree that they'll spend money on getting the best quality clothes for their kids. They're outdoor types, so they want to build a really good backyard play area.

The dream list doesn't include costs. It's their wish list—it can and will be changed; more than anything else, it's a way for them to look at who they are, and what they imagine will be their lives as parents. Don't forget—these early lists are "talking points," and their value is that they're a way to focus on your goals, a way to start the process of prioritizing, which will continue when you do start putting in dollar figures. Otherwise you run into the worst enemy of a budget or a financial plan: The situation in which whatever happens first gets the allocation, even though it may not be the most important.

Sue and Dan Worksheet 1: Dream List

DREAM	HIGH PRIORITY	IF THINGS WORK OUT
EDUCATION		
Private preschool	✔	
Private elementary school	✔	
Private high school		
College		
ENRICHMENT — COURSES, CLASSES		
Art		
Music, dance	✔	
Sports		✔
Languages		✔
Computer skills		✔
Summer camp	✔	

(continued on next page)

DREAM	HIGH PRIORITY	IF THINGS WORK OUT
CHILD CARE		
Live-in nanny	✔	
Regular day care		
TRAVEL		
Summer vacation trips		✔
Disney World		✔
Foreign travel		✔
FOR THE PARENTS—TIME ALONE		
Baby-sitter once a week	✔	

(continued on next page)

DREAM	HIGH PRIORITY	IF THINGS WORK OUT
THINGS TO BUY		

1

Starting Out as a Financially Aware Parent

You may bring your baby home from the hospital into a world of soft blankets and bright, cheerful mobiles hanging from the ceiling, but you're also bringing him home into a world of paperwork, documentation, and record keeping. Here's a checklist of a few things that you'll want to have in place.

Social Security Number

Why bother, for a little baby? Especially when who knows whether there'll still be a Social Security system by the time she grows up, let alone grows old?

Actually, you have to get your baby a Social Security number. Under current law, children must have one by the time they reach one year old, because you must use their Social Security numbers when you claim them as dependents on your income tax return. Also, this is the identifying number that you'll use to report unearned income on Uniform Gifts to

Minors Accounts (UGMA) and Uniform Transfers to Minors Accounts (UTMA) accounts, or any interest, dividends, or investment gains to the IRS. You'll need a Social Security number if you're going to open a bank account for your child, and probably if you're going to take out insurance for him/her.

A Social Security number is a good basic, if informal, ID, and babies have relatively few of them. Unless your baby has a passport, the birth certificate with footprint is probably the only real legal ID.

The whole process of getting a Social Security number may well have already been taken care of in the hospital. A lot of hospitals are now making a Social Security number application a part of the birth certificate process—this is the trend today, and more and more hospitals are doing it.

Otherwise, you'll have to apply for it, which you do by filing Form SS–5 at your nearest Social Security Administration office (if you're not sure where it is, you can call 1-800-772-1213 for information). In order to get your baby a Social Security number, you'll need his birth certificate and a second form of ID—a birth announcement in the paper is satisfactory.

A Social Security number costs you nothing.

Wills and Guardianships

As soon as you become a parent, a will becomes a real necessity, even if you're young and healthy and don't want to think about it right away.

Even if you don't have a lot in the way of assets, it's still a necessity. A will is where you'll name a guardian for your child, should anything happen to you; even if there's nothing else involved, this is tremendously important. For your child's future, and for your own peace of mind, you have to have the guardian issue settled. And if you're not convinced this is important, consider this—in some states, if you die without having named a specific guardian, the courts can take your children and place them in foster homes.

Further, if you have assets—and this includes an insurance policy—your will is where you'll make provisions for how they'll be used to provide for your children. This generally means creating a trust—your assets will then pay for your children's upbringing as long as they're minors. You do not have to appoint the same person or persons to be guardian of your children and trustees of your estate.

A will should be drawn up by a lawyer. A simple will does not require a specialist, and should be relatively inexpensive (under $500—perhaps even a good deal less—in most parts of the country); it may be worth shopping around a little if the fee seems too high. There are how-to books and even computer programs that are designed to help you draw up your will. These are great for research on the subject, and for helping you decide what you want, but I believe you should always have an attorney to make sure everything is legal and proper.

You might want to consider drawing up a living will at the same time. This isn't directly related to your kids, but someday it could be very important to them, if they need to know what you would want at that stage of life when extreme medical intervention is called for. Living wills can give someone else a power of attorney to decide what health care is appropriate for you if you're no longer able to decide for yourself, or designate a health care proxy who is authorized to make sure that the directives in your living will are followed.

The forms and regulations for living wills vary from state to state, so here again, you may want to consult an attorney. *The Living Will Handbook,* by Alan D. Lieberson, M.D., J.D., FACP (Hastings House, 1991), is a complete guide to the subject, including state-by-state forms for making your own living will.

I'll be discussing wills and guardianships in detail in a later chapter. For now, as you make up this checklist, make sure you know where you stand on this issue, and if you don't have a will that reflects your new status as a parent, make sure you get one.

Insurance

There are two branches to the insurance questions you'll want to ask yourself when baby makes three. First, do you have insurance? Second, what modifications do you need to make to your own insurance? And third, what about insurance on the baby? Is it a good idea? And if so, what would you need? I'll be discussing insurance questions in detail in Chapter 10: Making Provisions.

Savings Plans

Your savings plan should be in line with what your dreams are for the future, which means, of course, what your dreams are for your family. For example, when your children are ready for college, you'll want to be sure you have enough money to take care of that obligation, and that it's liquid when you need it to be.

And you also have to think about what else you want your family life to be, what other experiences you want your kids to have. If you're using an investment advisor, you can bring out your dream lists and show them to her. Perhaps she can show you where some of those variable expenses can become possible dreams.

I'll discuss savings and investment plans at greater length in a later chapter.

Family Strategy

Anyone who's ever gotten married knows that the one thing a young couple never has any shortage of is advice. Somehow, everyone seems to think you need it, and who knows, they may be right. You'll get advice on decorating, on how to make a great pot of coffee, on how to survive the first argument and how to deal with your in-laws. You'll get all sorts of financial advice, too, on investments and business opportunities, on how much harder it is for young folks nowadays, and how much easier it is for young folks nowadays. One piece of advice that you're almost guaranteed to get is this one: "Remember, if you wait until you can afford to have a baby, you'll never have one."

Like all the rest of the advice, that last piece is partly true, partly not. The point your uncle (or whoever) is trying to make is: If you want to start a family, start it. If you want a baby, that's the most important thing. You'll find some way to make ends meet.

But if you decide that you do want to wait until you can afford it, that doesn't mean you have to wait forever. It means you have to decide what you mean by "until you can afford it." How much money does it cost to raise a child? Two children? What will you want to have settled in your life before you start raising children?

The real danger comes if you decide you'll wait to have children until you can afford them and you never make a plan, so you never know exactly what "afford a baby" means. But the reverse of that coin is true, too. It's dangerous to decide you want a baby right away, or within two years, and then not create a financial strategy around that decision.

The Time Line

One of the basic tools you can use in making these decisions—and a key tool for using this book—is the time line.

A time line is simply a projection of where you want to be in the future . . . five, ten, fifteen, twenty years down the road. It factors in your projected income, your projected expenses, your projected family plans.

All of these items are subject to change, so your time line should be, too. The concept is flexible, it's designed to be tailored to your life, and the changes you go through. Don't make up a time line when you're 23, put it in a drawer, take it out when you're 43 and be surprised to find that your projections were off. Nobody's life ever goes according to plan . . . if it did, you should really begin to worry. So the time line is a very useful tool, but only if you keep adjusting it. You should expect to sit down and remap your time line at least once a year—more often, if a major change occurs in your life.

Here's our first time line. It's a simple one, but important. In it, we are keying on the birth of the baby: what you should have done before the baby is born, what you should do as soon as the baby is born.

Your Baby: Before and After

⇦ Baby ⇨	
Make/revise will Make savings/investment plan	Get Social Security number

My family plans certainly didn't materialize even remotely along the lines I had mapped out for them. When I was 23 years old, my time line called for two children (I had hoped for a girl and boy), spaced two years apart, the first at age 25. This was going to fit in perfectly with my career time line— the children would be born after I'd finished my training program, and I would still be well placed for moving up the corporate ladder at Chase Manhattan. And, of course, I planned to remain married to my husband; he'd be out of law school by then, and we'd have a two-parent, two-income family.

Well, eight miscarriages later, I had my first child at 31. After a couple more miscarriages, I had my second child three years later (they were a girl and a boy, but I can't attribute that to my great planning). My husband and I split up just after Rhett, our youngest, was born. Those years, and the ensuing years, have called for a great many adjustments to my time line—but having made the time line, and making adjustments on it, has meant that I always knew where I was and what I had to do.

Don't forget—this is *your* time line, so it needs to fit your needs and wants. That means you'll start with the line that's most important to you, and work everything else around it.

The first crucial distinction is between:

(a) people whose most important priority is to have kids on a defined schedule—right away, or within five years, or whatever. These people have to balance the rest of their wants against the financial realities of those babies, and the ripple effects those babies will have across their financial waters.

(b) people who want to have babies someday, but not just yet—"After everything else is in place." If you construct a time line that shows you making (and saving) a certain amount of money over a period of time, it will give you a chronology for what you want to have in place and when you want it in place. Then you don't have to get caught in the "if you wait until you can afford a baby you'll never have one" trap. You'll know when it's the right time to start that family.

Because the time line is such a flexible tool, you can always start with a dream list first. Why not? Start with everything you want, and you can pare back from there, making intelligent decisions, reasoned compromises, where you have to.

In each chapter of this book, we'll create detailed time lines for all the major needs and expenses you'll encounter in bringing children into this world and raising them. But to start out, let's look at the big questions: your income(s), when you want to have children, how many children you want to have, what your plans for shelter and education are.

Remember . . . decisions about having children are among the most personal, emotional decisions you'll ever make, and you certainly don't have to make them based on money alone.

But you should understand the financial ramifications of the decisions you do make.

A time line is the basis of a long-range plan, and a long-range plan is a vision. As you start making it, you're building a vision. You're visualizing yourself in the future, the way you want to be; and once you have that image, you can look back—from the top down, instead of from the bottom up. You can see how you got there, and with that long view, you can see all the intermediate steps in between.

This gives you a chance to make your major decisions in life proactive, not reactive. It gives you a better chance of making your dreams come true.

Starting the Process

Here's a worksheet you can use to start the decision-making process toward buying a home, starting with the projected size of your family—and this is, of course, an approximation. These things are rarely planned exactly, and when they are, real life rarely conforms to those plans. But most of us have a general idea whether we want a large or small family, whether we want to start right away or wait a few years. And remember, you can always revise your plan (whoops, sorry—there I go again).

If you're part of a couple, separately fill out the checklist below (Projected Family Size). Fill out the whole worksheet first, and then compare notes. If you haven't talked about these things before, you may have some surprises in store.

If you're a single parent, this is still an important checklist to fill out. The difference, of course, is that your vote is the only one; your decisions are yours alone.

For each item, mark your choice on the basis of how important it is to fulfill your wish in this area. Use the following scale:

0 = I really don't want this
1 = I never think about it
2 = I could be talked into it
3 = I have moderate interest
4 = I would really like this
5 = I don't see how I could live without it

For worksheets that include a "Total" column, add the two figures together to arrive at the total figure. But—and this is important—don't always make a decision based on the total alone. If one partner enters a zero next to a possibility—"I really don't want this"—then it should absolutely not be considered, even if the other partner sort of likes it. Conversely, if one partner enters a "5—I don't see how I could live without it"—then that should be the first choice you consider as a couple, and the one you make your top priority to achieve. Of course, if you have one partner who "really doesn't want" something that the other "can't live without," then it's time for some real negotiating.

Projected Family Size Checklist

	PARTNER 1	PARTNER 2	TOTAL
HOW SOON DO YOU PLAN TO HAVE YOUR FIRST CHILD?			
Have child(ren) already*			
Pregnant already			
Within 2 years			
2–4 years			
More than 4 years			

(continued on next page)

	PARTNER 1	PARTNER 2	TOTAL
HOW MANY CHILDREN DO YOU PLAN TO HAVE?			
One			
Two			
Three or more			
HOW FAR APART DO YOU PLAN TO SPACE THEM?	PARTNER 1	PARTNER 2	JOINT**
(Fill in number of years)**			

*If you have children already, this part of your time line is already set and not subject to revision; it will be a fixed part of all your future plans. There's no point assigning a number value to your choice—you don't have a choice. Otherwise, the 0–5 number should reflect the degree of importance this item has in your plans.

**For this item, write down the number of years each of you considers the optimum space between children, not the 0–5 number. Also note that the last column is a Joint figure, an average of your two choices, not a Total figure, as above, where you add the two figures together.

You'll start the time line like this:

1996	1997	1998	1999	2000	2001
	baby		baby		baby

Now, let's put you into this picture. Start with a projection of where you see yourself in the next ten years.

Projected Job/Career Line

	PARTNER 1	PARTNER 2
Are you working now? (Yes or no)		
Do you plan to work after the birth of your baby?* (Check preferred choice)		
Will not quit work at all		
Short parental leave (6 months maximum)		
Will take off 2–3 years to be with baby/babies		
Plan to work part-time		
Plan to work at home		
Plan to be full-time parent		
Do you have a job or a career?		
Do you see yourself as... (Check preferred choice)		
Extremely ambitious?		
Moderately ambitious?		

*A 1990 study by the Institute for Women's Policy Research, in Washington, D.C., estimated that the average earnings lost by American women who gave birth, in the year of birth and the two subsequent years, was $14,400 (in 1986 dollars). This is, of course, a figure that can vary widely. It depends not only on the mother's earning capacity and the mother's desire and/or ability to go back to work, but also health. Some women can work up to the last month of pregnancy, some women—and some pregnancies—require early bed rest.

	PARTNER 1	PARTNER 2
5 years from now, do you see yourself . . . (Check preferred choice)		
Working in the same place?		
Working in the same field?		
Do you have a career that requires further education? (Yes or no)		
Do your long-term plans include . . . (Check preferred choice)		
Working for a large corporation?		
Working for a small company?		
Working for yourself?		
Realistically, how much money do you expect to be making . . . (Check preferred choice)		
In 5 years?		
In 10 years?		
In 15 years?		
Priorities more focused on home than work?		

Once you start planning a family, you're creating a ripple of decisions that may very well affect your employment plans. I'll discuss this subject in more detail in a later chapter, but here are some of the questions you may want to start asking about your employment situation.

Career/Employment and Family

	PARTNER 1	PARTNER 2
DOES YOUR CURRENT PLACE OF EMPLOYMENT OFFER:		
A comprehensive health plan?		
Maternity/paternity leave? (Make sure your job is covered in the plan)		
Child care?		
Work-at-home provisions?		

Shelter

I'll be dealing with this subject in more detail in Chapter 4, but for now, let's just consider a few questions on a preliminary shelter worksheet.

Shelter

Will you be able to raise your child(ren) in the house you currently live in? (Yes or no) (If not, you'll definitely need to fill out the worksheets in Chapter 4 before you complete your time line.)	

IF NOT, HOW MUCH MORE WILL YOUR SHELTER EXPENSES BE?	CURRENT EXPENSE	ESTIMATED NEW EXPENSE	ADDITIONAL EXPENSE (difference between current and new)
Down payment			
Mortgage payments/ rent (per year)			
Taxes (per year)			

IF YOU DO CONTINUE IN YOUR CURRENT HOUSE, WILL YOU NEED TO REDO A ROOM FOR A NURSERY OR BUILD A NEW ADDITION? (Yes or no)	

IF SO, WHAT WILL THE ESTIMATED EXPENSES BE? (This is broken down into materials and labor, so you can figure the cost whether or not you plan to do the work yourself.)	MATERIALS	LABOR
Carpentry		
Electrical work		
Painting/wallpapering		
Plumbing		
Other		

How Much Does It Cost?

To make an initial family planning time line, you need to rough out figures in three general areas:

How many babies do you want to have, and when do you
want to have them?
How much money do you expect to be making?
What will the cost be of having a child?

If you're among the fortunate few, these figures will all balance out, and you'll discover that you have absolutely nothing to worry about. If you're like most of us, these figures are likely to need some adjusting. Think about putting off starting your family, try to see some way to increase your income, or find ways to reduce the budget for bringing children into the world and maintaining them.

We'll make up a complete worksheet and time line for this in the next chapter.

Sue and Dan

Here's how Sue and Dan filled out these worksheets.

Sue and Dan: Projected Family Size Checklist

	SUE	DAN	TOTAL
HOW SOON DO YOU PLAN TO HAVE YOUR FIRST CHILD?			
Within 2 years	4	4	8
2–4 years	5	5	definite

	SUE	DAN	JOINT
HOW MANY CHILDREN DO YOU PLAN TO HAVE?			
Two	4	4	8
HOW FAR APART DO YOU PLAN TO SPACE THEM? (Fill in number of years)	2	2	2

This is one area in which they didn't have much trouble. Both Sue and Dan had the same wants when it came to starting a family.

Sue and Dan: Projected Job/Career Line

	SUE	DAN
Are you working now? (Yes or no)	yes	yes
Do you plan to work after the birth of your baby? (Check preferred choice)		
Short parental leave (6 months maximum)	✔	✔
Plan to work part-time?		?
Do you have a job or a career?	Career	Job
Do you see yourself as... (Check preferred choice)		
Extremely ambitious?	✔	
Moderately ambitious?		✔
Priorities more focused on home than work?		?

(continued on next page)

	SUE	DAN
5 years from now, do you see yourself . . . (Check preferred choice)		
Working in the same place?	no	no
Working in the same field?	yes	yes
Do you have a career that requires further education? (Yes or no)	yes	yes
Do your long-term plans include . . . (Check preferred choice)		
Working for a large corporation?	✔	
Working for yourself?		✔
Realistically, how much money do you expect to be making . . . (Check preferred choice)		
In 5 years?		
In 10 years?		
In 15 years?		

Sue and Dan: Career/Employment and Family

	SUE	DAN
Does your current place of employment offer:		
A comprehensive health plan?	yes	yes
Maternity/paternity leave? (make sure your job is covered in the plan)	yes	no
Child care?	no	no*
Work-at-home provisions?	no	no*

*Dan notes: "If I go into business for myself, all these things are likely to change—including the fact that if I'm working out of my home, some of the child care will be provided by me!"

Sue and Dan: Shelter

Will you be able to raise your child(ren) in the house you currently live in? (Yes or no) (If not, you'll definitely need to fill out the worksheets in Chapter 4 before you complete your time line.)	no

IF NOT, HOW MUCH MORE WILL YOUR SHELTER EXPENSES BE?	CURRENT EXPENSE	ESTIMATED NEW EXPENSE	ADDITIONAL EXPENSE (difference between current and new)
Down payment	$0	$25,000	$25,000
Mortgage payments/ rent (per year)	$30,000	$18,000	($12,000)
Taxes (per year)	$0	$5,000	$5,000

If you do continue in your current house, will you need to redo a room for a nursery or build a new addition? (Yes or no)	no*

*Sue comments: "In a rented city apartment, we wouldn't be able to do much except buy baby furniture."

2

Conception to Birth

We all tend to think about that little breath of new life in the delivery room, that tiny new creature behind the glass of the hospital nursery, that baby cooing up at you from the changing table, as the beginning of the story. But every mother-to-be who's ever griped to her husband, around the seventh month, that he should have to carry Junior for a week or two, knows that the beginning of the story definitely comes earlier. And anyone who's ever been through it can tell you that the changes in your pocketbook show up . . . oh, a lot earlier.

We find out more and more, all the time, about the importance of prenatal care—and prenatal care means medical expenses.

A baby needs a lot of things you don't have around the house. Some of those things get passed from friend to friend and relative to relative, but some of them have to be bought.

Then there are unusual expenses which aren't common to everyone, but which *can* happen to anyone. Having a baby—conceiving a baby, then carrying it to term—isn't always easy, and sometimes it can be expensive.

Prenatal Medical Expenses

Your first expenses will be the medical ones surrounding your prenatal care and the delivery of the baby, and while there are various considerations here, the most important are:

Who will you choose as your health care provider?
Where do you want the baby to be delivered?
What kind of insurance plan do you have?

Choosing a Health Care Provider

WHAT KIND OF HEALTH CARE PROVIDER DO YOU WANT TO DELIVER YOUR BABY?	
Doctor (M.D.)	
Midwife	
CHOOSING A DOCTOR	
What is the doctor's fee?	
What is included?	
What is not included?	

PAYMENT (QUESTIONS FOR THE DOCTOR)	
Do you take our insurance plan?	
What insurance plans do you take?	
What are your payment arrangements?	
Do you take assignments (will you allow us to delay payment until the insurance company has paid the claim)?	
CHOOSING A MIDWIFE (IN ADDITION TO THE ABOVE QUESTIONS)	
Are you certified? (Only certified midwives are permitted hospital privileges)	

NOTE: Take this with you when you go to talk to potential health care providers.
Worthwhile source: The American College of Nurse-Midwives (ACNM) Directory of Nurse-Midwifery practices, available from the ACNM national office, (202) 289-0171.

Choosing a Facility

WHERE DO YOU WANT YOUR BABY TO BE BORN?	
Hospital	
Home birth	
CHOOSING A HOSPITAL	
How much does it cost?	
How close to you is it?	
What options does it have for childbirth?	
Does your doctor have privileges there?	

Beyond medical expenses is the money you have to lay out for supplies and equipment before the baby is born. These items can vary widely in price, depending on your taste and budget: from thrift and secondhand stores to the top of the line. You'll have to price these items yourself, but here's a worksheet that itemizes what you'll need to spend money on.

You'll start to need maternity clothing during your second trimester, so here's a list of what you'll need.

Prenatal Expenses—Supplies and Equipment: Clothing for Work

ITEM	QUANTITY		PRICE
	SUGGESTED	NEED TO BUY	
Loose jackets	1–2		
Dresses or jumpers	1–2		
Shirts to match jumpers	2–3		
Tops/blouses	4		
Low-heeled shoes	1–2		
Pants	1–2		
Maternity bras			
Maternity pantyhose	3–4		
Maternity panties	4–6		
Maternity slip	1		
Sweater/coat	1		
TOTAL			

Prenatal Expenses—Supplies and Equipment: Clothing for Home

ITEM	QUANTITY		PRICE
	SUGGESTED	NEED TO BUY	
Jeans/pants	2–3		
Shorts/sweats	1–2		
Tops	3–4		
Low-heeled shoes	1		
Sneakers	1		
Swimsuits	1		
Exercise outfits	1		
Sleepwear	1–2		
Sleep bras	1–2		
Liners/sanitary napkins	1 box		
TOTAL			

Before your first baby is born, you'll need to furnish a nursery. Again, prices for all these items can vary widely, from expensive designer outfits to hand-me-downs.

Prenatal Expenses—Supplies and Equipment: Nursery

ITEM	NEED TO BUY?	PRICE
Bassinet/cradle		
Infant carrier		
Crib and mattress		
Crib bumpers		
Baby bath		
Changing table		
Diaper bag		
Stroller/carriage		
Nursery monitor		
High chair		
Playpen		
Rocking chair		
Clothes hamper		
Decorations (pictures, mobiles, etc.)		
TOTAL		

ITEM	QUANTITY		PRICE
	SUGGESTED	NEED TO BUY	
Disposable diapers (1 month supply)	300–350		
Cloth diapers	4 dozen		
Waterproof pants (for cloth diapers)	4		
Undershirts	6–10		
Pajamas	4–6		
Stretchies/onesies	4–6		
Blanket sleepers	3		
Sweaters	2		
Drawstring gowns	4–6		
Bibs	2–4		
Caps	2		
Bunting	1		
Sunsuits	2		
Socks/booties	4		
Crib sheets	4–6		

(continued on next page)

ITEM	QUANTITY		PRICE
	SUGGESTED	NEED TO BUY	
Crib blankets	2		
Crib bumpers	1		
Mattress pads	1–2		
Receiving blankets	4–6		
Waterproof crib sheets	1–2		
Portable crib/carriage sheet	1		
Washcloths	6		
Bath towels	4		
Hooded bath towels	2–3		
Diaper bag	1		
Car seat	1		
TOTAL			

Starting Your Time Line

You'll be developing this time line during the course of the book as you create new data to put into it. I'll start it here with the three numbers you've estimated so far (and remember, these numbers are always subject to revision). I'll give you a worksheet to consolidate the numbers first, and then we can start transferring them to a time line.

1. How many children do you want, and when do you want to have them?

2. How much will it cost you to have a baby? Note that this will probably change in your time line estimate from baby to baby. Some costs, like medical costs, will be the same—or more, given rising costs of medical care—for each birth. Others, like baby clothes and furnishings, may go down—you can recycle a lot of those items from your first baby. Shelter-related costs may go down (you won't have to remodel a room for the nursery again), or they may go way up (at some point, your family size may dictate buying a larger house).

3. How much money do you expect to have at a given point in your future (such as at the birth of a baby or the year you buy a house)?

You'll need one more piece of information before you can finish filling out this consolidation worksheet: How much tax are you going to have to pay on your income? Tax laws change constantly, so you'll have to check with your accountant (or your copy of the tax code, if you do your own) as you revise these worksheets, but here is the 1995 tax rate, the one I'll be using for Sue and Dan:

1995 Income Tax Rate

TAX RATES	SINGLES	MARRIED/ JOINT	HEAD OF HOUSEHOLD
15%	$ 0–23,350	$ 0–39,000	$ 0–31,250
28%	23,351–56,550	39,001–94,250	31,251–80,750
31%	56,551–117,950	94,251–143,600	80,751–130,800
36%	117,951–256,500	143,601–256,500	130,801–256,500
39.6%	Over 256,500	Over 256,500	Over 256,500

The consolidation worksheet is where you gather together the numbers for your major expenses, so that you can see them at a glance.

I'll walk you through the details of it as we develop it for Sue and Dan.

Consolidation Worksheet I

(number of children you plan to have)	CHILD #1	CHILD #2	CHILD #3	CHILD #4
EXPENSES				
Medical (from pages 21–22)				
Objects (baby clothes, furniture, etc.) (from pages 23–27)				
TOTAL BABY EXPENSES				
Shelter (from page 14)				
Total current expenses*				
TOTAL EXPENSES				
Income (from page 12)				
Estimated taxes				
NET INCOME				

*Obviously, you are spending some money already, unless you're living at home with parents who are way more indulgent than any parents ought to be. Total up your existing expenses per year—existing shelter, food, clothes, transportation, debt service, etc.—and put that figure here.

Time Line 1

	1996	1997	1998	1999	2000
Total current expenses					
Total baby expenses*					
Total shelter expenses					
TOTAL EXPENSES					
TOTAL (NET) INCOME					
SAVINGS					

*Baby expenses should be put in the expected year of the birth of each baby you plan to have.

Now, for each prospective baby you have the beginnings of a budget. If your estimated figures show that you can afford the baby, then there's no problem. You can go ahead with your plans—remembering that circumstances can change, and these figures must be regularly reestimated and updated. If you're coming up short, then you've got to revise your plans to bring one or another figure in line: find some way to increase your income, find some way to cut down on your expenses, or consider postponing having your baby.

Special Expenses

Nothing in life ever goes according to plan. It's important to remember, though, that that doesn't mean you shouldn't plan; it means that you need to be flexible, able to restructure your plans.

Many of the changed plans regarding the children in our lives—and the children we want to bring into our lives—are dramatic and unexpected. Some changed plans can be painful. And many of them are costly.

Perhaps the first unexpected . . . and painful . . . expense comes if you find yourself unable to conceive a child.

This can mean either infertility or miscarriages, which are a financial as well as an emotional burden. They must be budgeted for in terms of medical expenses and lost time, just like a pregnancy. And it can mean alternative strategies for bringing a baby into your lives: fertility programs or adoption.

Fertility Programs

Fertility programs are expensive, and they don't have a guarantee of success. Most women do not succeed in becoming pregnant on their first attempt. So, before entering this area, you should not only consider whether you can afford to try a program once, but whether you can afford to repeat it—and how many times you can afford to repeat it. There's no way of knowing how many attempts it will take before you succeed in getting pregnant, and carrying to term, or even if you'll succeed, but in general, the older you are, the more attempts you are likely to need. There are currently no standards of reporting for infertility clinics, which leads to widely differing statistics for their effectiveness (one study reported that only 6 percent more women deliver a baby after fertility treatment than those who go untreated; another claimed an 85–90 percent success rate for fertility drugs).

The treatment options fall into two categories: low-tech and high-tech. The high-tech options are considerably more expensive—and women who have failed to get pregnant by low-tech methods are less likely to succeed with high-tech methods, too.

Low-tech options are:

Drug therapy, including clomiphene citrate (Clomid, Serophene), gonadotropin-releasing hormone (GnRh), human chorionic gonadotropin (hCG) (Profasi, Pregnyl, API), and menotropins (Pergonal).

Artificial insemination: placement of sperm directly inside the body.

Certain types of *surgery*, for example, blocked fallopian tube.

High-tech options include:

In-vitro fertilization (IVF): The egg is removed from the female and placed in an incubator with the male sperm to be fertilized before being placed in uterus.

Gamete intrafallopian transfer (GIFT): Eggs and sperm are placed in the fallopian tube to be fertilized naturally.

Zygote intrafallopian transfer (ZIFT): Already fertilized egg is placed in fallopian tube.

Tubal ovum transfer: Egg(s) are taken from ovary and placed in uterus to be fertilized naturally through intercourse.

Embryo transfer: Donor egg(s) artificially inseminated with father's sperm and fertilized egg(s) are placed in the mother's uterus.

Choosing a Clinic/Fertility Doctor (Reproductive Endocrinologist)*

Whether you decide to use a private physician or a clinic (you may want to interview both), find out the answers to all these questions.

QUESTIONS TO ASK A PRIVATE PHYSICIAN	
What training do you have? (Should be OB/GYN with further training in reproductive endocrinology)	
Do you specialize in a certain kind of treatment? What kind?	
What is your success rate? (Be sure to ask for live births, not pregnancies)	
QUESTIONS TO ASK A CLINIC	
Who is on staff? (OB/GYN, reproductive endocrinologist, urologist, etc.)*	
Are you affiliated with a teaching hospital? (The most successful clinics are)	
Do you offer counseling services in case of miscarriage or other fertility-related emotional problems?	
Do you offer preconception counseling?	
What is your success rate? (Be sure to ask for live births, not pregnancies)	
What is your experience? (Look for a clinic that has treated at least 100 people altogether, or at least 35 per year)	

*An IVF clinic staff should include: a reproductive endocrinologist, an experienced infertility surgeon, an experienced embryologist, an ultrasonographer or an OB/GYN with experience in this specialty, and a program director who is an M.D. It is also advantageous, but not essential, to have on-site obstetrical care.

SOURCE: "The High Cost of Fighting Infertility," Phillip Godwin, *Changing Times*, March 1989.

Not all insurance companies cover all infertility procedures, and some cover none. Some state regulations require that insurers provide some coverage (generally low-tech); most don't. Always find out what is covered by your plan and what, if any, lifetime or yearly cap exists. Even in states where coverage is mandatory, there are certain exceptions—always check to make sure you are covered for the procedure you want.

If you're covered by a company health plan, always get your company's permission in writing before going ahead. Sometimes a procedure will be covered because it is a standard OB/GYN treatment.

Here's a typical financial case history of one woman's attempt to get pregnant over a period of ten months— (8/93–4/94), using low-tech methods. She is 42 years old, living in a small Northeastern town, a physical therapist, and in good health. She is 4' 11½" tall, which means she needs smaller drug dosages than a larger woman would.

8/24/93	Office visit	$150.00
	Lab	15.00
9/08/93	Medical tests	535.00
9/15/93	Office visit	40.00
	Post-coital test	105.00
	Sonogram	165.00
9/21/93	Sonogram	165.00
9/28/93	Sonogram	165.00
	Lab	15.00
10/06/93	Endometrial preparedness	72.00
12/27/93	Estradiol	104.00
	FSH	67.00
	Sonogram	165.00
	Lab	15.00
12/28/93	Pergonal	581.27
	Syringes	6.41
12/30/93	Estradiol	104.00
	Progesterone	61.00
	Sonogram	165.00
	Lab	15.00

12/31/93	Hormone treatment	185.00
1/04/94	Estradiol	104.00
	Progesterone	165.00
	Sonogram	165.00
	Lab	15.00
1/05/94	Insemination (I/U)	185.00
2/02/94	Sonogram	165.00
2/21/94	Sonogram	165.00
2/25/94	Sonogram	165.00
	Estradiol	104.00
2/28/94	Estradiol (x2)	208.00
	Progesterone	61.00
	FSH	67.00
3/02/94	Insemination (I/U)	185.00
	Sperm washing	65.00
3/17/94	Endometrial preparedness	76.00
4/20/94	Sonogram	165.00
	Lab	15.00
	Hospital lab	666.00
4/26/94	Pergonal	581.27
	Syringes	6.41
	Sonogram	165.00
	Lab	15.00
4/28/94	Sonogram	165.00
4/29/94	Sonogram	165.00
TOTAL		$6392.05

She was pregnant after the second insemination, but at the end of April, she miscarried. The doctor recommended that she wait three months before trying again. In August of 1984, after completing the same procedure, she became pregnant again.

She was insured through a group plan at work, and the policy has paid 80 percent of all but her $15.00 lab tests.

Here's another case—something that happened to close friends of mine about ten years ago and involved a high-tech option: in-vitro fertilization. IVF was still a very new procedure then, and it was only offered in a few places. Brenda and Hank went to England for their procedure. They had been told it would cost $25,000, and they had budgeted the money.

They had not been told the whole story—$25,000 was the cost of the procedure, assuming that it worked the first time. It didn't include extras, like transportation and housing, which turned out to be not inconsiderable, especially since the procedure didn't work the first time, and they couldn't try again right away. What was worse, Brenda's menstrual cycle was now all messed up, and she had to wait until she could be fertilized again. Since it wasn't clear how long this waiting period would be, she had to stay in London the whole time, which turned out to be a month. The couple was committed to making this work, to conceiving and bearing a child. Brenda stayed in London for the month, which meant time lost from work, hotel bills, and living expenses. Hank went back to the States and his job, but he had to make several trips to London to be with her for what turned out to be false alarms.

The bills mounted. Later, Hank and Brenda told me that they didn't know if they ever would have started this project if they had known there was a possibility it would cost so much. But they were in the middle of it, and there was no backing out. They sold everything . . . they borrowed money . . . they ended up spending over $100,000.

The story has a happy ending. Hank and Brenda have a beautiful daughter now. But they're still paying off that debt.

Resources for Infertility

RESOLVE, Inc.
5 Water St.
Arlington, MA 02174
(800) 662-0106

Support group for infertile people

American Fertility Society
1209 Montgomery Highway
Birmingham, AL 35216-2809
(205) 978-5000

Has listings of member physicians and clinics—not a referral or recommendation service

Getting Pregnant: What Couples Need to Know Right Now
Niels H. Laursen, M.D., Ph.D., and Colette Bouchez
Ballantine Books, 1992 ($12.00)

The American Fertility Clinic also provides an excellent bibliography for books on fertility and adoption (complete with informative one-paragraph descriptions of each book), which they will send you, free. They also have a series of their own pamphlets available for $1 each, as well as a monthly journal, *Fertility and Sterility*.

Adoption

There are so many different kinds of adoptions, it's hard to put a figure on what it's likely to cost, but if you're choosing this route, check it out carefully. Private adoption agencies charge an average of $10,000, which often includes lawyers' fees. Some adoption agencies specialize in the adoption of foreign-born babies (see bibliography below), and the costs here vary widely. If you're interested in adopting an American-born child, a good place to start is:

The National Committee for Adoption
1930 17th St. NW
Washington, D.C. 20009-6207

This organization also publishes *The Adoption Fact Book*, $20.80, a comprehensive source of statistics, regulations, and facts on adoption in the United States.

Here's a list of some other literature on various aspects of adoption, as compiled by the American Fertility Society (descriptions from the society's *Reading Material* guide)

Adoption: A Handful of Hope
Suzanne Arms
Celestial Arts, Berkeley, CA, 1990. $12.95.

"A lengthy but readable text covering many facets of adoption, including the anxieties of waiting to adopt as well as the problems which may arise in raising adoptive children. This is not, however, a text of 'how to' proceed through the adoptive process. Highly recommended for couples considering or undergoing the adoptive process."

Family Bonds: Adoption and the Politics of Parenting
Elizabeth Bartholet
Houghton Mifflin, New York, NY, 1993. $21.95.

"This well-organized book is written for people struggling with some of the issues encountered in their journey through infertility, and ultimately adoption. Based on the author's personal experience with international adoption, it provides pros and cons, potential pitfalls to avoid, information on counseling programs, and a very well-organized approach to the 'home study.' This book is a 'must' for couples considering international adoption."

The Adoption Resource Book (Third Edition)
Lois Gilman
HarperCollins, New York, NY, 1992. $11.00.

"This book is essential to any couple planning to undergo adoption. The adoption process is explained thoroughly, including legal matters, the home study, preparation for a child, cost, and references. Discusses adoption scams and explains how to research a potential agency or attorney. Contains a state adoption directory as well as other references."

A book I would particularly recommend is *The Adoption Resource Book.*

Adopting After Infertility
Patricia A. Johnson
Perspectives Press, Indianapolis, IN, 1992. $21.95.

"Couples planning adoption after infertility treatment will find this book quite valuable. Throughout the book, the author emphasizes the importance of communication between partners and offers several valuable guidelines for maintaining a healthy relationship during a sometimes stressful process. Another section provides a 'battle plan' with good resources to help couples select a proper adoption process. The intricate aspects of confidential and open adoptions are fully described. Excellent resource for couples planning to pursue adoption."

The Adoption Directory
Ellen Paul, ed.
Gale Research, Inc., New York, NY. $55.00.

"An extensive reference text which covers such specifics as state statutes, adoption agencies, adoption exchanges, foreign requirements and agencies, independent adoption services, foster care and biological alternatives. Extremely well organized and indexed . . . more geared to agencies and institutions that regularly provide information to adoptive parents."

Adopt the Baby You Want
Michael R. Sullivan and Susan Schultz
Simon and Schuster, New York, NY, 1990. $18.95.

"A well-written and well-organized guide to adoption which, from the beginning, encourages prospective adoptive parents to consider their motivations and expectations. Thought-provoking questions and decision-making checklists make the format instructive yet friendly."

Loving Journeys Guide to Adoption
Elaine L. Walker
Mail order only: Loving Journeys, PO Box 755, Peterborough, NH 03458. 1992. $27.95.

"Part one begins by describing the basic prerequisites agencies and social workers expect of prospective adoptive parents, including conditions of the home, age requirements, and health and financial status. Part two is a directory . . . of state-by-state listings (with a few exceptions) of public and private adoption agencies and adoption attorneys. The directory is an excellent resource for persons who don't know where to begin or for anyone interested in the adoption process."

Your city or state department of social services can give you a list of licensed adoption agencies in your area.

Some companies (for example, Procter & Gamble and Time Warner) grant maternity leave and other benefits to families who adopt children. If you're considering going this route, and working for a company that grants maternity/paternity leave to adoptive parents, check it out.

Consolidation Worksheet 2

This is specifically for those people who have experienced difficulty in getting pregnant, and are exploring alternate methods.

(number of children you plan to have from Worksheet 1)	CHILD #1	CHILD #2	CHILD #3	CHILD #4
EXPENSES				
Medical *(from pages 21–22)*				
Medical (fertility treatments)				

(continued on next page)

(number of children you plan to have from Worksheet 1)	CHILD #1	CHILD #2	CHILD #3	CHILD #4
Adoption expenses				
Objects (baby clothes, furniture, etc. *(from pages 23–27)*				
TOTAL BABY EXPENSES				
Shelter *(from page 14)*				
Total current expenses				
TOTAL EXPENSES				
Income *(from page 12)*				
Estimated taxes				
NET INCOME				

Time Line 2

	1996	1997	1998	1999	2000
Total current expenses					
Total baby expenses					
Total shelter expenses					
TOTAL EXPENSES					
TOTAL (NET) INCOME					
SAVINGS					

Sue and Dan

Sue and Dan were lucky; they had no fertility problems. So they were able to fill in the simpler Consolidation Worksheet 1 and Time Line 1.

Here's what Sue and Dan's worksheets for this chapter look like. I won't be filling out every worksheet in this book for Sue and Dan, just those that will help illustrate the process. I've included Sue and Dan's worksheets for choosing a health care provider and facility, in spite of the fact that they're mostly personal preference questions (for example, doctor or midwife?) because they do have some numbers in them (the cost of a health care professional and facility) that Sue and Dan will need to fill out their consolidation worksheets.

Sue and Dan: Choosing a Health Care Provider

WHAT KIND OF HEALTH CARE PROVIDER DO YOU WANT TO DELIVER YOUR BABY?	
Doctor (M.D.)	✔
Midwife	
CHOOSING A DOCTOR	
What is the doctor's fee?	$2800
What is included?	prenatal/delivery 6 months postpartum
What is not included?	complications
PAYMENT (QUESTIONS FOR THE DOCTOR)	
Do you take our insurance plan?	yes
What insurance plans do you take?	
What are your payment arrangements?	⅓ — ⅓ — ⅓
Do you take assignments (will you allow us to delay payment until the insurance company has paid the claim)?	no
CHOOSING A MIDWIFE (IN ADDITION TO THE ABOVE QUESTIONS)	
Are you certified? (Only certified midwives are permitted hospital privileges)	

Sue and Dan: Choosing a Facility

WHERE DO YOU WANT YOUR BABY TO BE BORN?	
Hospital	✔
Home birth	
CHOOSING A HOSPITAL	
How much does it cost?	$5000
How close to you is it?	12 miles
What options does it have for childbirth?	natural
	assisted
Does your doctor have privileges there?	yes

Sue and Dan: Prenatal Expenses—Supplies and Equipment: Clothing for Work

ITEM	QUANTITY		PRICE
	SUGGESTED	NEED TO BUY	
Loose jackets	1–2	1	$50
Dresses or jumpers	1–2	1	60
Shirts to match jumpers	2–3	2	40
Tops/blouses	4	3	75
Low-heeled shoes	1–2	1	60
Pants	1–2	1	25
Maternity bras		3	45
Maternity pantyhose	3–4	4	20
Maternity panties	4–6	6	30
Maternity slip	1	1	25
Sweater/coat	1	1	125
TOTAL			$555

Sue and Dan: Prenatal Expenses—Supplies and Equipment: Clothing for Home

ITEM	QUANTITY		PRICE
	SUGGESTED	NEED TO BUY	
Jeans/pants	2–3	2	$40
Shorts/sweats	1–2	1	10
Tops	3–4	3	45
Low-heeled shoes	1	1	60
Sneakers	1	1	75
Swimsuits	1	1	80
Exercise outfits	1	1	80
Sleepwear	1–2	2	60
Sleep bras	1–2	2	40
Liners/sanitary napkins	1 box	—	—
TOTAL			$490

Sue and Dan: Prenatal Expenses—Supplies and Equipment: Nursery

ITEM	NEED TO BUY?	PRICE
Bassinet/cradle	shower	—
Infant carrier	1	$120
Crib and mattress	1	700
Crib bumpers	1	80
Baby bath	—	—
Changing table	shower	—
Diaper bag	shower	—
Stroller/carriage	1	250
Nursery monitor	1	65
High chair	1	120
Playpen	1	200
Rocking chair	1	150
Clothes hamper	1	35
Decorations (pictures, mobiles, etc.)	shower	—
TOTAL		$1720

ITEM	QUANTITY		PRICE
	SUGGESTED	NEED TO BUY	
Disposable diapers (1 month supply)	300–350	—	—
Cloth diapers	4 dozen	4 dozen	$300
Waterproof pants (for cloth diapers)	4	4	40
Undershirts	6–10	20	50
Pajamas	4–6	6	90
Stretchies/onesies	4–6	6	90
Blanket sleepers	3	3	60
Sweaters	2	2	60
Drawstring gowns	4–6	5	75
Bibs	2–4	4	30
Caps	2	2	20
Bunting	1	1	40
Sunsuits	2	2	20
Socks/booties	4	4	30
Crib sheets	4–6	6	70

(continued on next page)

ITEM	QUANTITY		PRICE
	SUGGESTED	NEED TO BUY	
Crib blankets	2	2	45
Mattress pads	1–2	2	30
Receiving blankets	4–6	6	50
Waterproof crib sheets	1–2	2	20
Portable crib/carriage sheet	1	—	—
Washcloths	6	6	25
Bath towels	4	4	35
Hooded bath towels	2–3	2	40
Car seat	1	shower	—
TOTAL			$1220

Sue and Dan Consolidation Worksheet 1

	(number of children you plan to have from Projected Family Size Checklist)			
EXPENSES	**CHILD #1**	**CHILD #2**	**CHILD #3**	**CHILD #4**
Medical	$7800	$7800		
Objects (baby clothes, furniture, etc.)	3985	2265		
TOTAL BABY EXPENSES	11785	10065		
Shelter				
Total current expenses				
TOTAL EXPENSES				
Income				
Estimated taxes				
NET INCOME				

Sue and Dan's medical expenses are $2,800 for the doctor's fee (Choosing a Health Care Provider) and $5,000 for hospital expenses (Choosing a Facility). They expect these figures to be the same for each child. Baby clothes and accessories will be less for the second child, because they'll still have some of what they bought for the first one.

Sue and Dan Time Line I

	1996	1997[1]	1998[2]	1999[3]	2000
Total current expenses	$25,000	$25,000	$30,000	$50,000	$55,000
Total baby expenses	0	11,785	0	10,065	0
Total shelter expenses[4]	30,000	30,000	30,000	23,000	23,000
TOTAL EXPENSES	55,000	66,785	60,000	83,065	78,000
TOTAL (NET) INCOME	73,200	76,860	80,520	84,810	86,800
SAVINGS	18,200	10,075	20,250	1,115	8,800

1. Baby born in this year
2. Add $5,000 for cost of infant
3. Projected move this year
4. Figuring out shelter costs will be discussed in detail in Chapter 4.

3

Family Strategies and Your Job

Not many American lives are predictable anymore; not many follow a straight line. I went to work for Chase Manhattan Bank mostly because I couldn't type and because I had made an indelible impression by the spectacular way I botched my interview; I don't recommend botching an interview as the best way to get a job, but on this one occasion, it worked for me. At the time, I was still a halfway hippie and wasn't admitting to my friends that I'd taken a job with the Establishment.

When I became president of The First Women's Bank I had to fight off an attempt by certain members of the board to fire me when they found out I was pregnant. And when I was a divorced mother with two young children and was entering a phase of my life where I probably really could have used the security of a nice solid bank behind me, I became an entrepreneur, starting my own business on a shoestring.

My experience was unique, but not untypical—in fact, it was typical in its uniqueness. Everyone has a story today, and everyone's story is different. It's the rare individual, or the rare couple, who has a predictable life, staying in one place, the wife staying at home and the husband going to work, like Dagwood Bumstead—and, like Dagwood, working for Mr. Dithers for fifty years.

Most people move. They change jobs. They look for opportunities to better themselves. They even change careers. And they don't always plan these terrifically important life decisions to dovetail with a strategy to match that other crucially important life decision—having a family.

You don't live in a world where changing jobs or careers is unheard of. So why not think about it now, while you're thinking about the best strategy for raising a family?

Thinking About Your Job Future

Use the next three worksheets to determine your best possible future career choices. For each item, mark your choice on the basis of how important it is to fulfill your wish in this area. Use the same scale as before, with a figure representing each of your individual opinions, and add the two to make the total. Remember that a 5 or a 0 from either partner is an absolute "must have" or an absolute veto.

  0 = I really don't want this
  1 = I never think about it
  2 = I could be talked into it
  3 = I have moderate interest
  4 = I would really like this
  5 = I don't see how I could live without it

Where Do You Want to Live?

	PARTNER 1	PARTNER 2	TOTAL
East Coast			
Mid-Atlantic			
South			
Midwest			
Southwest			
Northwest			
Pacific Coast			
Big city			
Suburbs			
Small city			
College town			
Small town			
Rural			
Overseas			
Build career around home location			
Build home location around career			

The next two worksheets involve individual choices, not partnership choices, so there's no need for a "Total" column.

How Important Are the Following in Choosing a Job/Career?

	PARTNER 1	PARTNER 2
Liberal maternity/paternity leave		
Liberal sick leave		
Day care provided		
Not much travel		
Not much overtime		
Regular hours		
Flexible hours		
Can take work home		
Can primarily work out of home		
Can work part-time with benefits		
Can work part-time		

Feelings About Your Current Job

	PARTNER 1	PARTNER 2
It's what I want to do for the next 20 years		
It's what I want to do for the next 5 years		
I would change careers if it improved my quality of life		
I am looking to change careers now		

Flexible Workplace Policies

The Women's Bureau of the U.S. Department of Labor provides extensive information on work options. I've adapted the following from information they provide. If one or both of you are thinking about working part-time after the baby is born, or staying home for a while and then going back to work, think about these options, then find out if your current employer offers any of them—or if another potential employer in your field does.

Part-time employment: The official Bureau of Labor Statistics definition of this is less than thirty-five hours per week. It can be either temporary or permanent, it can be a specified number of hours per day, days per week, or weeks per month.

The advantage is that you work fewer hours and have more time to spend at home with your kids. Disadvantages can include a lower pay rate and fewer benefits (even prorated), or no benefits at all.

Voluntarily reduced worktime: If you're an experienced and valued employee in a company, you may be able to work out this variation on part-time work, which enables employees to reduce their work time and salary by a specified amount (usually anywhere from 5 percent to 50 percent), for a specified period (say, six to twelve months) or permanently, while retaining benefits and seniority on a prorated basis. This can be a desirable alternative if you don't want to change jobs, and if you can work it out with your current employer.

Job sharing: Two (or more) workers share the duties of one full-time job, each working part-time; or two or more workers who have unrelated part-time assignments share the same budget line. This can be divided up in all sorts of ways—you and the person you're sharing with can share all aspects of the job, and just split up the time; or you can split up the responsibilities as well.

Some common ways of sharing time on the job are:

- Splitting daily hours
- Alternating days
- Alternating weeks in a biweekly pay period

This tends to be more of a "real job" than the average part-time job: vacation days, sick leave, and other benefits are split as well. Some companies base vacation leave on seniority and assume the full cost of health and dental coverage.

Flexible leave policies: On a full-time job, accrued sick and annual leave can be combined for employees' use as they choose. Policies may also include paid or unpaid personal leave time.

Flexitime: A work schedule that allows employees to vary their arrival and/or departure times, as long as they work a prescribed number of hours during a pay period, and are present during a daily "core time."

This can be very useful in helping you create a schedule that allows you to be available to your kids at certain key times. It may also mean that you, or someone, will have to make sure that schedules are coordinated so that the workplace duties are covered at all times.

The federal government began using flexitime as an experiment in 1979; the program was permanently authorized by Congress in 1985. It has become one of the most popular alternative options in the private sector, too.

Flexiplace-Telecommuting: Workers perform duties at home or at a satellite work site and are usually connected to their offices through a computer and/or a telephone.

If the kind of work you do lends itself to this approach, it can be an excellent choice. You should make sure that you know whether employee benefits, workmen's compensation, etc., apply to your telecommuting job. And don't forget that you're going to owe your employer quality time and work; just because you're at home, doesn't necessarily mean that you won't need a baby-sitter.

Compressed work week: This is any work schedule that enables a full-time employee to work the equivalent of a full week in less than five days, or two weeks in less than ten days.

Telephone access: Some workplaces that have stringent rules about use of the telephone have relaxed those regulations to allow working parents to receive calls from family members at any time, and to make calls to children, baby-sitters, or other caregivers.

Maternity/Paternity Leave

The Family and Medical Leave Act of 1993 requires employers to provide workers with up to twelve weeks of unpaid leave per year for the birth or adoption of a child, or for the foster care of a child, or to care for the illness of a child, spouse, or parent, or because of an employee's own illness. This is a good thing for families, but it shouldn't be your only consideration on this issue. For one thing, you may be able to do better. For another, it may not apply to you.

Companies with less than fifty employees are exempt from the provisions of the Family and Medical Leave Act. Certain exemptions are also made for "key employees." So before you start counting on your family leave, make sure that you actually have it.

By the same token, some employers do better than the federal guidelines—and there are some states that have laws on the books that are even stronger than the Family and Medical Leave Act. One piece of good news is that most of these laws are gender-neutral, but that's something else you might want to check for your state—or, if you're considering a move, the state you're considering moving to.

As of 1994, five states (Hawaii, Connecticut, Rhode Island, New York, and New Jersey) and Puerto Rico had temporary disability insurance (TDI) laws that provide partial salary replacements for non-work-related disabilities, including childbirth and pregnancy-related conditions.

The Women's Bureau of the U.S. Department of Labor (Washington, D.C. 20210) offers a booklet called "State Maternity/Paternity Leave Law" that offers a state-by-state breakdown of laws on this matter.

You'll want to check with your employer—or prospective employer—about the company's disability and maternity leave policies. And remember that sometimes, in some pregnancies, you'll need maternity leave before the baby is born, too.

I did, with Rhett. I went into premature labor . . . *really* premature. Rhett was due in December of 1985; I was admitted to the hospital in October. They stabilized the labor, but they told me I'd have to stay in bed if I wanted to carry the baby to term. Not only in bed, but in the hospital. Not only in the hospital, but in the intensive care unit.

Careerwise, it wasn't a good time for me. I had just taken

over the presidency of The First Women's Bank in July. The First Women's Bank was a troubled institution, and it needed as much intensive care as I did. As it turned out, one of the things they were troubled about was my condition. Being pregnant did not sit well with the board of directors.

I was able to juggle both lives—an invalid and a bank president—only by means of some very fast talking. Normally, they're not going to let you have a telephone and a typewriter and a bunch of files in an ICU, but I managed to get the rules bent enough to accommodate me, and I kept the bank afloat while I waited for my wonderful baby.

But this was, I'll point out again, unusual. Having to go to bed for weeks, even months, in order to save a baby is not the norm, but it does happen. And if it happens to you, you don't want any surprises at work or from your insurance company.

Leaves, Benefits, and Other Programs

You'll want to make sure you know exactly what your employer's policies are on all of these. Use this checklist to make sure you've covered everything.

What Does Your Employer Cover?

DEFINITION	DOES EMPLOYER/ PROSPECTIVE EMPLOYER COVER?
LEAVE	
Disability leave for childbirth: Medical leave covering all pregnancy-related physical disability, including childbirth. This is not to be confused with parental or family leave.	

(continued on next page)

DEFINITION	DOES EMPLOYER/ PROSPECTIVE EMPLOYER COVER?
Child care leave for mothers/fathers/adoptive parents: Policy permitting an extended period of time off to care for a newborn, very young, or recently adopted child. Also called family leave or parenting leave. This is distinct from personal leave.	
Personal leave: Policy permitting time off for an extended period (weeks or months) that can be used for family reasons, such as care of a sick dependent. This is distinct from personal days policy or leave for military service or community service.	
Personal days: Policy permitting time off for short periods (days or hours).	
BENEFITS	
Dependent Care Assistance Plan (DCAP): Benefit enabling an employee to spend pre-tax dollars on dependent care costs.	
Adoption expenses: Subsidy related to adoption.	
Resource and referral (R&R) for child care: Provides information and counseling to employees in need of child care services.	
On- or near-site child care: Center-based child care located at or near the worksite (not part of a consortium).	
Consortium center: Child care sponsored by a group of collaborating employers.	

(continued on next page)

Definition	Does Employer/ Prospective Employer Cover?
Child care discounts: Company contracts with child care centers, reducing employees' costs by a standard percentage.	
Child care vouchers: Company subsidizes a portion of child care expenses at a provider chosen by the parent.	
Other Programs	
Employee Assistance Plan (EAP): Includes programs addressing family needs and concerns (for example, individual counseling for work/ family conflicts).	
Relocation services for families: Company-sponsored support programs for the families of relocated employees.	
Sick child care: Corporate foundation for dependent care provides, for example, specific training for supervisors in how to manage work/family issues.	
Unemployment insurance: Provided to people able and available to work, while unemployed through no fault of their own.	
Workmen's compensation: Benefits paid to injured employees or dependents of injured employees as a result of injury occurring in the course of, and as a result of, the employment.	

Sue and Dan

Sue and Dan completed the worksheets in this chapter, and here's what they found out about their feelings on their careers, and how they fit into their future plans. For the blocks that have been left out of their worksheet, they both put "1—I never think about it."

After they'd filled out the worksheet and checked the totals in the right-hand column, they had a guide to their mutually arrived at priorities. They looked first in the categories with the highest totals—with the exception of categories in which one of them put a 5 (unquestionably the first choice) or a zero (unquestionably not to be considered).

Sue and Dan: Where Do You Want to Live?

	SUE	DAN	TOTAL
East Coast	4	3	7
Mid-Atlantic	2	1	3
Northwest	1	3	4
Pacific Coast	1	3	4
Big city	3	0	0
Suburbs	4	2	6
College town	4	4	8
Small town	1	3	4
Rural	2	3	5
Build career around home location	0	3	0
Build home location around career	5	3	Settled

Sue wants to live on the East Coast. Her family is in the east, and she's close to them. Her career prospects are stronger in the east. But she's willing to consider moving, so she won't put an absolute 5 here. Fortunately, she doesn't have to. There are other parts of the country that appeal to Dan, but he's happy with the East Coast as well.

Sue wouldn't mind staying in the city, but Dan absolutely doesn't want to. There's no debate here—one zero equals a zero. They won't make long-term plans to live in the city.

They don't just put down numbers on a chart, of course. They talk all these things through. Sue says that a large part of her attraction to the city is its cultural attractions. She wants to live close enough so that she'll be able to make trips in for the theater, concerts, or museum days. When they have kids, she'd like to be able to expose them to the same benefits. Dan feels the same way. He realizes that's one of the reasons why a college town instinctively attracted him.

They both like the idea of a college town, so that will be the first place they'll look for a house when they're ready. The suburbs are an acceptable choice, as is a rural location. They'll look in a small town as a last resort, but they will consider it.

Sue does put a 5 next to "Build home location around career." She doesn't want to choose a place to live and then make a career move based on that. So this area doesn't go to a vote, either—the choice is settled.

Sue and Dan: Choosing a Job/Career

How Important Are These?	Sue	Dan
Liberal maternity/paternity leave	5	3
Liberal sick leave	3	3
Day care provided	4	4

(continued on next page)

How Important Are These?	Sue	Dan
Not much travel	2	2
Not much overtime	2	2
Regular hours	2	2
Flexible hours	2	4
Can take work home	4	4
Can primarily work out of home	1	4
Can work part-time with benefits	1	3 — (ha!)
Can work part-time	1	3

Sue and Dan, looking this over, notice that neither of them is enthusiastically oriented toward a job with regular hours, not much travel, and not much overtime. Unless one or the other of them rethinks this in the future, their plans are going to have to include proximity to child care and a space in their budget for it.

Dan is already thinking about going to work for himself, which explains the "ha!" next to "Can work part-time with benefits." He also realizes, as he fills this out, that he would consider working part-time and taking on more child care responsibilities.

Sue and Dan: Feelings About Current Job

	SUE	DAN
It's what I want to do for the next 20 years	3	1
It's what I want to do for the next 5 years	5	4
I would change careers if it improved my quality of life	1	4
I am looking to change careers now	0	1

Sue is very attached to her new career. Dan likes his—and probably wants to keep doing it for the next five years—but he's not convinced that something he likes more won't come along.

Of course, they both understand that once they've made a commitment to having kids, their children will come first, and that will influence every job and shelter decision they make. But all things being equal, they'll make it a priority to plan around Sue's career in preference to Dan's. Sue will work hard to ensure that her career choices include such factors as an enlightened workplace with liberal maternity/paternity leave and an understanding attitude toward working mothers.

4

Shelter

I've said that your financial decision-making is going to be affected by your children as soon as you start looking around for a Lamaze class, but for some decisions, even that's not early enough. The August 1994 issue of *Money* magazine profiles Tim Carlsen, a young, single investment banker in Seattle who is already making life decisions based on his plans for a projected future family: He's paying $1,000 a year to a matchmaking service, he's looking into buying a $200,000 condo for two, and he has $40,000 set aside, earmarked for the ring, wedding, and honeymoon.

The young banker may be planning, but the editors of *Money* suggest that his planning may be just slightly off the mark. I'd agree with them in principle—that he's right to be planning for the future, but that his plans are misdirected—although not in specifics.

Money's editors advise: Hold off buying a house until you find a mate.

A $160,000 mortgage on a $200,000 condo would cost about $19,000 a year in mortgage interest and property tax, and would save only $4,700 in income tax, calculates Susan Nelson, a local financial planner. But if Carlsen waits until he and his intended can pool their income and afford, say, a $240,000 mortgage on a $300,000 house, they could then save $7,000 in taxes.

The editors of *Money* may not have gone far enough. For a major decision like shelter, even an unmarried person, if he/she sees marriage and a family as a strong possibility for the near future, not only a future spouse but future babies can be part of the equation. Young Mr. Carlsen should not only be thinking about buying a house to live in, he should be thinking about what size house he's going to need, and when he's going to need it—and I absolutely agree that he should have these plans in place before he starts saving for a ring.

However, after long experience as a working single mom, I'd question whether you should be locked into making such major plans as buying a house—and even financing a family—based on having a partner. You don't have to be married to afford a home. In fact, even if you are married, you're not always well advised to plan on having two incomes. And not just because one of you may elect to stay home with the kids. People lose jobs. In Sue and Dan's case, when Dan eventually leaves his job to start his own business, there may be a period of time when he has no money coming in.

The important point here is that you have to make sure you have a plan, with carefully considered priorities.

Now, I want to reiterate a couple of things I've said before—and I may say them again, for that matter, partly because I'm a bit of a noodge and partly because they're really important:

First, it's important to have a long-range financial plan, but it's just as important to remember that it's not etched in stone tablets. It should help you plan your life; it shouldn't run your life. You can change it; you can be sure that it's going to change; in fact, you should sit down and revise it at regular intervals.

Second, remember that none of this is advice on how to run your life. It's information that can help you in considering your options. If, for example, putting off your first home until you're married makes you feel as though you're putting too much stock in the importance of a significant other—that it's diminishing your sense of self-worth—then by all means, get that perfect dream house for yourself.

OK . . . I promise not to make this point too many more times.

Starting the Process

Here's a worksheet you can use to start the decision-making process toward buying a home, starting with the projected size of your family—and this is, of course, an approximation. These things are rarely planned exactly, and when they are, real life rarely conforms to those plans. But most of us have a general idea whether we want a large or small family, whether we want to start right away or wait a few years. And remember, you can always revise your plan (whoops, sorry—there I go again).

If you're part of a couple, fill out this worksheet separately. Fill out the whole worksheet first, and then compare notes. If you haven't talked about these things before, you may have some surprises in store.

If you're a single parent, this is still an important checklist to fill out. The difference, of course, is that your vote is the only one; your decisions are yours alone.

For each item, mark your choice on the basis of how important it is to fulfill your wish in this area. You remember the scale:

0 = I really don't want this
1 = I never think about it
2 = I could be talked into it
3 = I have moderate interest
4 = I would really like this
5 = I don't see how I could live without it

Dream House Checklist

How important is each of the following to you?	Partner 1	Partner 2	Total
Room for each child			
Spare bedroom			
Home office			
Living room			
Family room			
Library/study			
Eat-in kitchen			
Dining room			
Laundry/mud room			
Gourmet kitchen			
Master suite			
Workshop			
Garage			
Outdoor play area			
Space to keep pets			

(continued on next page)

HOW IMPORTANT IS EACH OF THE FOLLOWING TO YOU?	PARTNER 1	PARTNER 2	TOTAL
Provision for disability			
Environmental considerations			
Other			

NOTE: Add as many other rooms—and, below, other factors—as you want. It's your dream list. This worksheet may also be a useful tool to take along with you when you actually start looking for a house. Once you have your joint priorities settled, hand it to your real estate agent—it'll save time.

Quality of Life

HOW IMPORTANT IS EACH OF THE FOLLOWING TO YOU?	PARTNER 1	PARTNER 2	TOTAL
Short commute to work			
Wide range of cultural/ leisure activities (city values)			
Neighborhood activities for kids (Suburban values)			
Rural life			

(continued on next page)

HOW IMPORTANT IS EACH OF THE FOLLOWING TO YOU?	PARTNER 1	PARTNER 2	TOTAL
Good public school			
Proximity to private schools			
Safe neighborhood*			
Proximity to day care			
Proximity to playgrounds			
Proximity to family			
Proximity to public transportation			
Proximity to shopping			
Proximity to medical facilities			
Other			

*A safe neighborhood is one in which your whole family has the perception of safety. For example, if either of you was raised in the city and is terrified of the dark, isolation and wild animals, then a secluded farmhouse will not feel like a safe neighborhood. NOTE: Here again, feel free to add as many "Other" quality of life items as are important to you.

Where are you and your partner on the same wavelength? Where are you different?

For the first part of the worksheet you'd better make sure you're in agreement. Talk these differences through, and come up with a tentative number for each item that you can both agree on. Put that number in the "Total" column.

For the second and third parts, if there's a difference between the two of you, enter the higher value in the "Total" column . . . for now. The first paradigm we're going to build is a "wish" paradigm.

Quality of Life

To build your wish time line, start with your "Quality of Life" list, and use this to build a *locus* for where you want to live.

Start with quality of life? Isn't this backward? Surely the other issues, like family planning and the kind of house you want, ought to come first?

But remember, you're visualizing now—you're starting from where you want to be, and looking back to how you got there. And quality of life issues are about the kind of life you want to have.

First, make a list of every quality of life item that rated a 5 from either of you (the items you can't do without).

Second, for each item, write down the distance you'd be willing to travel to take advantage of that item. This is a wish list, so the person who has assigned the high-priority rating to the item gets to choose the mileage. Where both have assigned the same high rating, then write down the shorter distance.

Get out a map of the area that you want to look in for your dream home. Actually, you'll probably end up needing a series of maps. A large road atlas will be a good place to start; once you're ready to focus on a specific area, you can get local maps from your chosen area.

Take a compass—the kind school kids use for geometry class, with a spike on one point and a pencil on the other. Now put the point of the compass on every point that's represented by a 5 for either of you on your Quality of Life list, or by a total of 8 for the two of you, and make a circle. The radius of the circle will be the number of miles you're willing to travel.

In other words, if you want to be within 60 miles of your parents, you'll need to put a 60-mile circle around their hometown. If you want to live within 125 miles of an urban cultural center, like San Francisco or Austin or New York or Washington, make a 125-mile circle around that city.

If you don't want to commute more than 60 miles to work, make a circle with your job as the center. (This assumes that you already have a job you're planning to stay in. If you're job hunting, this means creating another locus, and matching up the job and shelter loci.)

You may have particular needs. If you need a hospital that provides a specialized form of treatment and need to be within a hundred miles of it, you'd have to make a circle for that. If someone in your family is a gifted figure skater or equestrian and needs advanced lessons, perhaps you need to be within 25 miles of those facilities.

The locus is where all those circles intersect. That's the location where you can expect to be happiest; it's the location in which you should start your house search.

What if your circles don't intersect and there is no locus?

That's one of the beautiful parts of this system. You have to compromise, but that doesn't necessarily mean that one of you will have to give up some cherished quality of life ingredient. It can mean, instead, that you'll compromise on distance . . . you'll extend a circle. One of you will agree to commute 80 miles to work . . . one of you will agree to live 125 miles from Mom and Dad. The drive is a little farther, but you're still working toward the maximum enhancement of the quality of your life.

What you have created, so far, is a *macro-locus*. Now it's time to get inside that broader area, and create a *micro-locus*. This is when you bring out the county maps, town maps, city maps. This is when you zero in, when you fine-tune the location of the area where you want to live. Proximity to public transportation, shopping, a good pediatrician—do you have a special kind of day-care program you want to enroll your child in, like a Montessori nursery school? You can find out where they are within your macro-locus, and use them as compass points in finding the neighborhood, town, or rural area you want.

Your Dream House

This one is even simpler. All you need to do is put together the highest numbers you have in your "Total" column, and you have a picture of your dream house.

You have a detailed picture of your dream house already, in fact—more detailed than you'll need right away. For now, just add up the number of 8's or better in your "Total" column, and you'll have the size of your house.

In this next worksheet, you can start putting preliminary numbers together. You have the size of your dream house; you have some idea where you want to live. In the worksheet, you'll do what photographers call "bracketing an exposure." When they want to capture a beautiful landscape or a smiling face perfectly, they'll take three pictures—one with the lens set for what they think is the perfect amount of light, one with the lens opened up a little in case they guessed low, and one with the lens closed down a little in case they guessed too high. You'll be looking for cost on houses that have just the right number of rooms. You can make a column for one more room—in case you can afford it, and in case you think of something else later. But you'll also make columns for one, two, or three rooms less—in case you have to scale back your dreams.

Then it's just a matter of looking in the real estate sections of the newspapers or the real estate marketing giveaways for the communities that fit your profile. Write in the names of the communities in the left-hand column, and the numbers of rooms in the top row. For each box in the matrix, enter the average cost for a house that size in that community. If you're looking at a larger community, like a city, you might want to break it down into neighborhoods: In Nashville, you'd make one row for Belle Meade and another for Goodletsville.

Your Dream House Cost Matrix

	__ ROOMS	__ ROOMS	__ ROOMS (optimum)	__ ROOMS
Community 1				
Community 2				
Community 3				
Community 4				
Community 5				
Community 6				
Community 7				
Community 8				
Community 9				

This is all part of the procedure of visualizing—starting where you want to be and then seeing how you got there. Of course, it's not the whole movie. But it is the hoped-for last reel, the place where music swells up and the credits roll over tearful, happy faces.

That image has you living in the perfect spot, in the perfect house, with the perfectly planned family.

The Money Issues

Now it's time to add your personal finances to the equation: what you (or the two of you) are making now, what your future career prospects look like. This worksheet is designed to help you get a picture not only of your salary, but of the place that work plays in your lives.

Projected Career and Money Plans

HOW IMPORTANT IS YOUR CAREER TO YOU?	PARTNER 1	PARTNER 2
Central part of life		
Important		
Just a job; could find another		
Would rather stay home with children		

HOW MANY INCOMES ARE THERE IN YOUR FAMILY?	
Two	
One (could be two)	
Single breadwinner household	

HOW MANY INCOMES DO YOU EXPECT TO HAVE AFTER YOUR CHILDREN ARE BORN?	PARTNER 1	PARTNER 2
Would like two		
Would like one		
Has to be two		
Has to be one		

DO YOU WORK AT HOME?	PARTNER 1	PARTNER 2
Yes		
No but could		
No, couldn't possibly		

INCOME/PROJECTED INCOME (enter $ amount)	PARTNER 1	PARTNER 2	TOTAL
How much do you make now?			
How much do you see yourself making?			
At birth of 1st child			
At birth of 2nd child			

SAVINGS (enter $ amount)	PARTNER 1	PARTNER 2	TOTAL
How much do you have saved?			
How much do you see yourself having saved at birth of 1st child?			
How much do you see yourself having saved at birth of 2nd child?			
How much do you currently save per year?			

CAREER MOBILITY	PARTNER 1	PARTNER 2
Could move if partner had to change location for a career advancement		
Could not move		

IS YOUR CAREER DEPENDENT ON BEING IN A CERTAIN LOCATION?	PARTNER 1	PARTNER 2
Will probably stay put		
Will probably move		
Move (if it happens) would likely be to certain locations (list)		

Putting It Together

You have to put a house into two very distinct places in your budget. First, you'll have to estimate the lump sum you'll be putting down in order to buy the house, and that has to be measured against your savings. Second, you'll need to know how much you're going to have to spend on an ongoing basis to keep the house, and that has to be measured against your income.

Here are a couple of worksheets that will help you in this part of the process. Later, following Sue and Dan, I'll show you how they filled out these worksheets, and some of their figures can be a rough guide to you in estimating yours; others, you'll just have to find out for yourselves. A down payment on a home, for instance, can fluctuate from zero percent (100 percent financing) to ... well, if you could lay your hands on a whole bunch of cash, you could buy the house straight out, with no mortgage.

Estimated Closing Costs and Funds Needed to Purchase

ITEM	DATA	AMOUNT
Purchase price		
Mortgage amount		
Mortgage type		
Years		
Down payment		

(continued on next page)

ITEM	DATA	AMOUNT
PAYMENT AMOUNT (PER MONTH)		
Mortgage		
Taxes		
Total		
Mortgage Application Fee		
Points (each point=1% of amount borrowed		
Bank attorney's fee		
Buyer's attorney's fee		
Mortgage tax (5% of the mortgage amount)		
PMI (PRIVATE MORTGAGE INSURANCE) REQUIRED IF BORROWING MORE THAN 80% OF VALUE		
Homeowner's insurance (fire, hazard, liability)		
Title insurance		
Tax escrow and pro-rated taxes		
Plot plan and survey		

(continued on next page)

ITEM	DATA	AMOUNT
Filing fees (mortgage and deed)		
Fuel adjustments		
Escrow setup charge		
Prepaid interest (covers interest until first mortgage payment)		
Structural tests		
Pest inspection		
Water inspection		
Septic inspection		
Radon inspection		
ESTIMATED CLOSING COST		
CASH DOWN PAYMENT		
TOTAL CASH NEEDED PURCHASE		

Prequalifying

Many banks and/or realtors will *prequalify* you for a mortgage. That is, they'll give you a worksheet that will enable you to figure out how much of a mortgage you'll qualify for—what kind of home you can afford. If you've been prequalified, it doesn't mean you're guaranteed to get a mortgage—it is all unofficial. People are taking your word for it that the numbers are accurate, and they'll all have to be verified before you officially qualify for a mortgage. Still, your prequalifying worksheet can give you an accurate idea of what you can actually afford

Prequalifying Part I

	METHOD 1	**METHOD 2**
Yearly gross income *(including usual/constant overtime and bonus)*		
Monthly gross income *(yealy income ÷12)*		
Adjustment percentage *(multiply monthly gross income by this frigure)*	x .28	x.36
Adjusted gross monthly income		
Long term monthly payments *(list all payments—only for Method 2)*		
NET MONTHLY INCOME *(Adjusted gross monthly income minus long term monthly payments)*		

When you fill out this part of the worksheet (a pocket calculator would be a good thing to have on hand at this point), you'll be using two different methods to arrive at your adjusted gross monthly income. Both are legitimate—in Method One the adjusted gross and net figures are the same; in Method Two, your gross figure will be larger, but then you'll subtract all your long-term monthly payments.

Long-term monthly payments are defined as any debt on which you still owe a year or more of payments, so here's a hint: If you're getting ready to apply for a mortgage, and you have a debt service—let's say, a car payment—on which you owe a little over a year's worth of payments, you might consider paying it down so that you only owe eleven months or less. That way it won't be considered as a continuing debt when you go to apply for your mortgage.

As you move on to the second part of this worksheet, the first figure you're going to use is the lower of the two net monthly income figures. The reason why you use the lower figure is that you're being as conservative as possible—you want to be sure that you're going to qualify for the mortgage you want.

Prequalifying Part II

TOTAL PITI* PAYMENT YOU CAN QUALIFY FOR (lower of the two net monthly income figures)	
APPROXIMATE MONTHLY FIRE/ HAZARD INSURANCE	
APPROXIMATE MONTHLY REAL ESTATE TAXES	
APPROXIMATE MONTHLY MORTGAGE PAYMENT	

*PITI = principal, interest, taxes, and insurance

You may need to do a little research—a local realtor in the area you're considering should be your best source—to find out what the approximate monthly insurance and taxes will be. You'll subtract those two figures from the total PITI payment to get your approximate monthly mortgage payment.

Next, figure out how much of a mortgage you qualify for, on the basis of how much of a monthly payment you can afford. Use the tables on pages 86 and 87.

Mortgage Rates—30-Year Mortgage

INTEREST RATES

MONTHLY PAYMENT	7%	7.5%	8%	8.5%	9%	9.5%	10%	10.5%	11%	12%	13%
$300	45,092	42,905	40,885	39,016	37,285	35,678	34,185	32,796	31,502	29,166	27,120
400	60,123	57,207	54,513	52,021	49,713	47,571	45,580	43,728	42,003	38,887	36,160
500	75,154	71,509	68,142	65,027	62,141	59,463	56,975	54,660	52,503	48,609	45,200
600	90,185	85,811	81,770	78,032	74,569	71,356	68,370	65,592	63,004	58,331	54,240
700	105,215	100,112	95,398	91,038	86,997	83,249	79,766	76,525	73,504	68,053	63,280
800	120,246	114,414	109,027	104,043	99,425	95,141	91,161	87,457	84,005	77,775	72,320
900	135,277	128,716	122,655	117,048	111,854	107,034	102,556	98,389	94,506	87,497	81,360
1000	150,308	143,018	136,283	130,054	124,282	118,927	113,951	109,321	105,006	97,218	90,400
1100	165,338	157,319	149,912	143,059	136,710	130,819	125,346	120,253	115,507	106,940	99,440
1200	180,369	171,621	163,540	156,064	149,138	142,712	136,741	131,185	126,008	116,662	108,480
1300	195,400	185,923	177,169	169,070	161,566	154,605	148,136	142,117	136,508	126,384	117,519
1400	210,431	200,225	190,797	182,075	173,995	166,497	159,531	153,049	147,009	136,106	126,559
1500	225,461	214,526	204,425	195,080	186,423	178,390	170,926	163,981	157,510	145,828	135,599
1600	240,492	228,828	218,054	208,086	198,851	190,283	182,321	174,913	168,010	155,549	144,639
1700	255,523	243,130	231,682	221,091	211,279	202,175	193,716	185,845	178,511	165,271	153.67
1800	270,554	257,432	245,310	234,097	223,707	214,068	205,111	196,777	189,011	174,993	162,719

INTEREST RATES

MONTHLY PAYMENT	7%	7.5%	8%	8.5%	9%	9.5%	10%	10.5%	11%	12%	13%
$300	33,377	32,362	31,392	30,465	29,578	28,729	27,917	27,140	26,395	24,997	23,711
400	44,502	43,149	41,856	40,620	39,437	38,306	37,223	36,186	35,193	33,329	31,615
500	55,628	53,937	52,320	50,775	49,297	47,882	46,529	45,233	43,991	41,661	39,518
600	66,754	64,724	62,784	60,930	59,156	57,459	55,834	54,279	52,789	49,993	47,422
700	77,879	75,511	73,248	71,085	69,015	67,035	65,140	63,326	61,587	58,325	55,325
800	89,005	86,299	83,712	81,240	78,875	76,612	74,446	72,732	70,386	66,657	63,229
900	100,130	97,086	94,177	91,395	88,734	86,118	83,752	81,419	79,184	74,990	71,133
1000	111,256	107,873	104,641	101,550	98,593	95,765	93,057	90,465	87,982	83,322	79,036
1100	122,382	118,661	115,105	111,705	108,453	105,341	102,363	99,512	96,780	91,654	86,940
1200	133,507	129,448	125,569	121,860	118,312	114,918	111,669	108,558	105,578	99,986	94,844
1300	144,633	140,235	136,033	132,015	128,171	124,494	120,975	117,605	114,377	106,318	102,747
1400	155,758	151,023	146,497	142,170	138,031	134,071	130,280	126,651	123,175	116,650	110,651
1500	166,884	161,810	156,961	152,325	147,890	143,647	139,586	135,698	131,973	124,983	118,554
1600	178,010	172,597	167,425	162,480	157,749	153,224	148,892	144,744	140,771	133,315	126,458
1700	189,135	183,385	177,889	172,634	167,609	162,800	158,198	153,791	149,569	141,647	134,362
1800	200,261	194,172	188,353	182,789	177,468	172,377	167,503	162,837	158,367	149,979	142,265

Where your approximate monthly mortgage payment shows up on the grid is the total mortgage you can prequalify for.

As I said before, there are all sorts of mortgages available, and a wide variety of possible down payments. However, an average down payment is 10 percent of the cost of the house. So if you divide the mortgage payment by .9 (sounds tricky, but with a calculator it's easy), you'll get the high end of the price range of the house you should be looking for.

Now, you're ready to plug in another set of figures: the estimated cost, per year, of your new home—the yearly payment for mortgage, taxes, and insurance. You can use your prequalifying figures as a guide—that represents the most you'll be able to spend. You can, of course, decide that you want a little more margin for emergencies, and that means you'll allocate less.

Estimated Cost Per Year, New Home

ITEM	% AMOUNT (per year)
Mortgage payment	
Taxes	
Insurance	
TOTAL	

Consolidation Worksheet 3

	Now	**Child #1**	**Child #2**	**Child #3**	**Child #4**
Years to planned birth					
EXPENSES					
Medical (no complications)					
Medical (fertility treatments)					
Adoption expenses					
Objects (baby clothes, furniture, etc.)					
TOTAL BABY EXPENSES					
Shelter (continuing cost) *(from page 88)*					
TOTAL CURRENT EXPENSES					
TOTAL EXPENSES					
INCOME *(from page 78)*					
Estimated taxes					

(continued on next page)

	Now	Child #1	Child #2	Child #3	Child #4
Net income					
Savings to date *(from page 79)*					
Projected savings per year					
Years to planned move					
Cash requirement from savings— down payment on house *(from page 82)*					

*This is the time when you rethink these figures. Compare your original estimates with the housing costs you've researched in the Quality of Life worksheet (pages 71–72). I there's a discrepancy, it's time to go back and reevaluate your earlier worksheets and time lines.

Notice that we've made a few additions to the consolidation worksheet. There's a new column, called "NOW." You're no longer just planning for the future; when you're figuring your income and your savings, you have to start with what you have, and what you're making, right now.

If you already have children, then the "Child 1" (or 2, or 3, depending on how many kids you already have) *becomes* the NOW column. You start with your current situation. One of the inescapable facts about having kids is that when you have them, you have to deal with them. You can't ask them to stay on hold for a year or two until you catch up with your master plan.

We've added a "Savings" row, and we've changed the "Income" row to the newer figures you've generated for this chapter. The theory here is that you're beginning to get a clearer sense, by now, of the real-life expenses associated with having children, and you're looking at your income and savings assumptions from a more realistic perspective.

Finally, we've added two more rows: "Cash Requirement," which is for the major expenses that you're going to have to pay for out of savings—buying a house and paying for college—and "Net Savings," which is your savings balance after it's drawn down by that cash requirement.

So make sure you notice, when you're putting your shelter expenses into this worksheet, that they go in two different places. Your ongoing shelter costs—rent or mortgage—are entered as "Shelter (continuing cost)," and are taken from the Estimated Cost Per Year, New Home worksheet (page 88) or from your rental expenses. Your one-time shelter costs —the down payment on a home and related costs—are entered as "Cash requirement from savings—down payment on house," and are taken from the Estimated Closing Costs and Funds Needed to Purchase worksheet (pages 80–82).

Time Line 3

	1996	1997	1998	1999	2000	2001
Total current expenses						
Total baby expenses						
Total shelter expenses (ongoing)						
TOTAL EXPENSES						

(continued on next page)

	1996	1997	1998	1999	2000	2001
TOTAL (NET) INCOME						
Savings rate						
SAVINGS TO DATE						
Cash outlay from savings						
NET SAVINGS						

If the set of figures in the *cash outlay from savings* box of your time line is higher than the set in the *total savings* box, then you'll have to start making adjustments—adjusting down the cost of your house, for example, or adjusting it farther down the time line until you're at a point where you *can* afford it. With this system, though, you have a clear-cut way of looking into your needs, and your figures, to start making the adjustments. You can look at these possible areas:

Money: Is there any realistic way you see yourself making more money? Here are some possibilities:

Career change
Change in location
Both partners working full-time
Reduce expenses
Find a way to save more

Locus: If you enlarge the locus, will it grow to include areas where real estate prices are lower? If so, here are the possibilities:

Stretch the mileage requirements for your "definites."
Stretch the mileage requirements for your 8's.
Eliminate some of your 8's.
Downgrade some of your definites.

Dream House: This one is simple—if you make your dream house smaller, you can keep the same earning capacity and ideal locus, and pay less for your home.

Baby-Planning Time Line: There's one more figure you can adjust: Perhaps if you postpone the schedule for starting your family, your ability to pay for shelter will catch up. If you're taking this option, make sure you readjust the time line to give you a clear target date.

Putting It Together, Part 2—How I Did It

In 1974, I made the first in a series of decisions that brought the following elements into focus: a time line (which was to be changed several times), a shelter locus, a career decision, all of which bore directly on financial plans and decisions.

It was time to buy our first home. I was doing well at Chase Manhattan; my husband would soon be graduating from law school; and we were starting to plan a family.

I had to be within commuting distance of New York City. John was in law school in New Jersey, and he would be practicing in New Jersey. My mother and sisters and grandmother lived in New Jersey.

We took out a map and started drawing circles. A short commute was very important to me, so we began with circles in a ten-mile radius from New York City. We checked schools, transportation, and real estate prices. The last presented an impasse. Houses were way beyond our range.

We kept drawing larger circles. We drew circles as well from my mother's and grandmother's and sisters' homes. We also had a list of the best school systems in New Jersey. We were planning to start a family right away, and we were looking for a house that we could keep for a long time, that would be big enough to raise two children in.

Just a little over 30 miles outside the city, our circles overlapped in an area we could afford, which had one of the best school districts in the state: the little town of Mountain Lakes. Transportation to the city was good enough, although not great. I decided to make that compromise, and we bought the cheapest house we could find that met our criteria, for $67,000.

We moved in, I commuted, and of course, things didn't go according to plan. We didn't have our first child until 1983, when Kyle was born. By 1985 I was divorced, with two children, and rethinking my whole life strategy.

I was still working in New York—now as president of The First Women's Bank—and I didn't want to commute anymore. I didn't want my kids to be that far away from me that much of the time. I had grown to love the house in Mountain Lakes, but it didn't make sense to live there now. I didn't know what the future would bring, so I decided not to sell the house right away. Instead, I rented it, and Kyle and Rhett and I moved into an apartment in New York.

I investigated the New York City school system, but decided on private school for the kids. My expense pattern was changing; commuting expenses were down, and so were property taxes—the rental of the house covered them. I had rent to pay on my city apartment and the expenses of the private schools. I also had the great cultural resources of New York City available to the kids, and I discovered that meant a great deal to me.

In 1989 I left the banking business and formed my own company, the Children's Financial Network. I was able to work out of my home, but most of my business was in New York. I bought an Upper West Side apartment.

In 1992, facing the high costs of private school, and no longer tied to New York for my work, I started rethinking the question of New York City *vs.* the suburbs. Once again, it was time for an analysis of alternatives.

THE CITY

If I stayed in the city, and continued to send the kids to their expensive and prestigious private school, I would be paying approximately $25,000 per year for their combined tuition, plus another $6,000 for their combined bus fare. Rhett was going into first grade, Kyle fourth grade, so that meant twelve more years for Rhett and nine for Kyle. Assuming a raise in tuition to $15,000 each after four years, and a raise in bus fare that would add an extra $250 each after four years, I was looking at:

TOTAL EXPENSE FOR KIDS' CITY SCHOOLING—12 YEARS: $357,250

Since one of the advantages of New York is cultural enrichment, I figured in—for theater tickets, museums, the ballet, etc.—about $1,000 per year for each of the children. So at twelve years for Rhett and nine for Kyle, that made an additional figure:

TOTAL EXPENSE FOR CITY ENRICHMENT—12 YEARS: $21,000

TOTAL FOR CITY: $376,250

THE SUBURBS

These were the expenses I'd incur by moving back to Mountain Lakes for the remainder of the kids' grade school careers. There would be commuting expenses for me. I'd have to drive into the city two or three times a week, a round trip of approximately 70 miles, and I'd have to park. Gas and tolls would come to about $25 per week, parking about $60. That would add up to $85 per week or $4,300 per year. Using a rough estimate of inflation, that figure would probably go up to $5,000 after four years. I estimated:

COMMUTING EXPENSES FOR NEALE—12 YEARS: $57,400

I'd also need a second car for the use of my child care provider (and later on, when the kids were old enough to drive and not need full-time child care, to use as a family car). With the help of a local mechanic, I figured $5,000 for a secondhand car, $700 for insurance, $1,000 a year for gas, and $600 for maintenance. That's $2,300 a year for upkeep. Assuming a used car, kept up well and driven sparingly, should last four years, that's $5,000 plus $9,200 for the first four years, a total of $14,200. If that figure rose, say, $1,000 for each subsequent car, the total would be:

SECOND CAR FOR FAMILY—12 YEARS: $46,600

I'd still want the cultural enrichment of New York City for the kids, although we'd go less often. I estimated 10 trips yearly, at $200 a trip, for a subtotal of $2,000 per year—again, twelve years for Rhett, nine for Kyle:

NYC ENRICHMENT, FROM SUBURBS—12 YEARS: $21,000

TOTAL FOR SUBURBS: $125,000

It made sense economically. Would a public school education in suburban New Jersey be equivalent to a first-rate New York City private school? I decided that in Mountain Lakes, it would. We had chosen the community in the first place for the excellence of its school system.

We moved back to the country that year.

Sue and Dan

Sue and Dan started by filling out their worksheets to get a sense of their overall wants and needs. They had planned to have their first child right away, and then two more, spaced out every three years, but reality intervened, and when Sue and Dan began looking for a home, they were 36 and 33 years old, with a 9-year-old and a 3-year-old.

They had made up a dream house checklist when they first started thinking about a family, and they modified it based on their new circumstances.

Sue and Dan: Dream House Checklist

HOW IMPORTANT IS EACH OF THE FOLLOWING TO YOU?	SUE	DAN	TOTAL
Room for each child	5	4	settled
Spare bedroom	3	3	6
Home office	2	5	settled
Living room	5	5	settled
Family room	5	5	settled
Library/study	4	2	6
Eat-in kitchen	3	3	6
Dining room	5	5	settled
Laundry/mud room	4	1	5
Gourmet kitchen	2	4	6
Master suite	5	5	settled
Workshop	1	5	settled
Garage	4	4	8
Other (Au pair room)	5	2	settled
Outdoor play area	4	5	settled

(continued on next page)

HOW IMPORTANT IS EACH OF THE FOLLOWING TO YOU?	SUE	DAN	TOTAL
Space to keep pets	0	1	settled
Provision for disability	1	3	4
Environmental considerations	4	4	8
Other			

Sue and Dan: Quality of Life Checklist

HOW IMPORTANT IS EACH OF THE FOLLOWING TO YOU?	SUE	DAN	TOTAL
Short commute to work	3	2	5
Wide range of cultural/ leisure activities (city values)	3	3	6
Neighborhood activities for kids (suburban values)	2	5	settled
Rural life	4	4	8
Good public school	5	5	settled
Proximity to private schools	0	0	settled
Safe neighborhood	5	5	settled
Proximity to day care	2	2	4

(continued on next page)

HOW IMPORTANT IS EACH OF THE FOLLOWING TO YOU?	SUE	DAN	TOTAL
Proximity to playgrounds	4	4	8
Proximity to family	4	2	6
Proximity to public transportation	5	3	settled
Proximity to shopping	3	4	7
Proximity to medical facilities	5	5	settled
Other			

Dan was ready to leave his job in the city and go into business for himself; Sue needed to commute, so they began looking at the suburbs close to New York City.

They wanted a community that had a good school district.

They wanted a house large enough so that Dan could run a home office out of it. He'd only need a room big enough for a computer, desk, and filing cabinets in the home, but that room was crucial. And he'd need a storage area for supplies.

They wanted a place that would be large enough to afford them the option of live-in child care.

They looked at communities like Tuxedo and Dobbs Ferry, New York; Short Hills, New Jersey; Greenwich, Connecticut. The sort of house they wanted listed for around $300,000—far outside the price range they had intended.

Sue and Dan: Dream House Cost Matrix

	8 ROOMS	10 ROOMS	12 ROOMS (optimum)	___ ROOMS
Community 1 Tuxedo, NY	$280,000	300,000	330,000	
Community 2 Dobbs Ferry, NY	350,000	375,000	450,000	
Community 3 Newburgh, NY	125,000	135,000	180,000	
Community 4 New Paltz, NY	100,000	135,000	175,000	

At the same time, Sue and Dan filled out the series of Projected Career and Money Plans worksheets, to complete their home-buying financial profile.

Sue and Dan: Projected Career and Money Plans

HOW IMPORTANT IS YOUR CAREER TO YOU?	PARTNER 1	PARTNER 2
Central part of life	✔	
Important		
Just a job; could find another		✔
Would rather stay home with children		

HOW MANY INCOMES ARE THERE IN YOUR FAMILY?	
Two	✔
One (could be two)	
Single breadwinner household	

HOW MANY INCOMES DO YOU EXPECT TO HAVE AFTER YOUR CHILDREN ARE BORN?	PARTNER 1	PARTNER 2
Would like two	✔	✔
Would like one		
Has to be two		
Has to be one		

DO YOU WORK AT HOME?	PARTNER 1	PARTNER 2
Yes		
No, but could		✔
No, couldn't possibly	✔	

INCOME/PROJECTED INCOME (enter $ amount)	PARTNER 1	PARTNER 2	TOTAL
How much do you make now?	$85,000	$35,000	$120,000
HOW MUCH DO YOU SEE YOURSELF MAKING?			
At birth of 1st child	91,000	35,000	126,000
At birth of 2nd child	200,000	50,000	250,000

SAVINGS (enter $ amount)	PARTNER 1	PARTNER 2	TOTAL
How much do you have saved?			15,000
How much do you see yourself having saved at birth of 1st child?			100,000
How much do you see yourself having saved at birth of 2nd child?			200,000
How much do you currently save per year?			18,200

CAREER MOBILITY (check appropriate box)	PARTNER 1	PARTNER 2
Could move if partner had to change location for a career advancement		✔
Could not move	✔	

IS YOUR CAREER DEPENDENT ON BEING IN A CERTAIN LOCATION? (check appropriate box)	PARTNER 1	PARTNER 2
Will probably stay put	✔	n/a
Will probably move		
Move (if it happens) would likely be to certain locations (list)		
Chicago		
Philadelphia		

They went back to their locus. They didn't want to settle for a house that would be unsatisfactory for their needs. This meant that they'd have to start drawing larger circles.

Sue's mother lived in upstate New York, north of the city, so they decided to focus in that direction. Their next circle included the small town of New Paltz.

They looked at each other. They had driven through the area. It was appealing: apple orchard country, the majestic Hudson River, the beautiful Shawangunk mountains. It was a college town—that had been one of the possibilities on their early checklists—that meant, potentially, a lively cultural scene and a good school district.

New Paltz was within easy driving distance of Sue's mother in Middletown, and there was express bus service to New York City, which meant that Sue's commuting time would be no worse than it might be from locations closer to the city. Since she wouldn't have to drive, with a laptop computer, she could turn that time to productive use.

Sue and Dan made an appointment with Laurie Della Villa-Miller of PRG Realty in New Paltz. Laurie, a realtor with thirty years' experience in the Hudson Valley, described the home-buying process for me, and re-created an imaginary sequence of events leading to Sue and Dan's ultimately purchasing a home.

"We recommend that prospective home buyers drive around an area that they're interested in, getting the feel of it, and just spend time looking at the range of housing possibilities there are in that area," Laurie told me. "It's a good idea, while you're doing that, to look at the realtors' signs that are up outside houses you like. If one realtor seems to be listing a lot of those houses, that may be the one you should go to. Of course, a realtor can show any house, and she'll have access to information on the homes in the county or counties if she subscribes to the Multiple Listing Service, but you may find that a broker who has listed a lot of the sort of home you like may have a special feeling for that sort of home. So Sue and Dan may have found us that way, or they may have seen an ad for one of our listings in the *New York Times*, or they may have been referred to us. In any case, let's say they called and made an appointment for the next Saturday morning.

"On their first visit, if they're like most prospective buyers, they were expecting to jump in the car and go out and start looking at homes. Instead, we invited them to sit down and become acquainted, so that ultimately we'd be streamlining their home-buying process.

"We started, as we always do, by reviewing the New York State disclosure forms and defining the different roles that brokers can play in the transaction process: seller's agent, buyer's agent, broker's agent, or agent representing both seller and buyer—with the full and informed consent of both parties.

"We generally provide the client with a Needs and Wants form, but Sue and Dan already had theirs made up, so we were able to look at it and start thinking about the kind of house they'd want.

"But first we made sure that they knew all the expenses that go into closing a deal on a house, so there'd be no surprises later on. We gave them a list of the expenses that they would have to expect to pay when it came to closing on a house . . . "

Down payment
Mortgage application fee
Points (each point equals 1 percent of amount borrowed)
Bank attorney
Buyer's attorney
Mortgage tax (.5 percent of the mortgage amount)
PMI (insurance required if borrowing more than 80 percent
    of value)
Homeowners insurance
Title insurance
Tax escrow and prorated taxes
Plot plan and survey
Filing fees (mortgage and deed)
Fuel adjustments

Escrow setup charge (charged by bank)

Prepaid interest (covers interest until first mortgage payment)

Tests and inspections (structural, water, septic, pest, etc.)

"We discussed the tax advantages of owning a home. Most people know that there is a tax deduction for the money you spend on interest and real estate taxes. We made sure Sue and Dan also knew about potential long-term tax advantages. You are responsible for paying taxes on any profit you gained when selling a home, but, under the current tax code, you may defer those taxes as long as you purchase another home of equal or greater value in a prescribed time period. People can and do purchase and sell home after home, making a profit on each sale and deferring taxes each time they sell.

"And if you sell your home after the age of fifty-five under the current tax code you may be eligible for a one-time 'age exemption' of up to $125,000 on the accumulated profits on the sales of your homes. This can be one of the best annuities you have!

"Finally, we began the process of prequalifying Sue and Dan. They had begun filling out the prequalifying worksheet; we helped them with information on insurance and tax rates in the various areas they'd be looking at."

Sue and Dan: Prequalifying Part I

	METHOD 1	**METHOD 2**
Yearly gross income *(including usual/constant overtime and bonus)*	$138,000	$138,000
Monthly gross income *(yealy income ÷12)*	11,500	11,500
Adjustment percentage *(multiply monthly gross income by this figure)*	x .28	x .36

(continued on next page)

	METHOD 1	**METHOD 2**
Adjusted gross monthly income	3,220	4,140
Long-term monthly payments *(list all payments—only for Method 2)*		
car		500
loans		1,000
NET MONTHLY INCOME *(Adjusted gross monthly income minus long-term monthly payments)*	**3,220**	**3,640**

Sue and Dan: Prequalifying Part II

Total PITI payment you can qualify for *(lower of the two net monthly income figures)*	$2,640
Approximate monthly fire/hazard insurance	32
Approximate monthly real estate taxes	425
APPROXIMATE MONTHLY MORTGAGE PAYMENT	**2,183**

"After filling out this form, Sue and Dan decided to call a local bank and speak to a mortgage officer to continue the preapproval process. They also planned to begin interviewing attorneys, and before the day was over, we took them to see a few houses that met their needs.

"By the next time Sue and Dan came to the office, they had met with a mortgage officer and been preapproved for a mortgage. Fortified by that knowledge, they looked at some more houses.

"Seeing a number of houses can begin to make a difference in the dream list you've put on paper. Sue had listed a garden as one of her wants, but suddenly, upon seeing a house with a large family garden area, she realized just *how* important it was to her. The house was a contemporary style, and Dan had always said Colonial was the only style he'd ever accept, but everything else about this place was so suited to their needs and tastes, he found himself feeling more flexible about style.

"They looked at a couple more houses before lunch. After a lunch break, though, they came back and asked if they could see that contemporary house with the large garden one more time.

"It was time to sit down and work up some numbers. We made up an estimated closing cost statement for them, based on the figure they planned to offer for the house . . ."

Sue and Dan: Estimated Closing Costs and Funds Needed to Purchase

ITEM	DATA	AMOUNT
Purchase price		$159,300
Mortgage amount		137,000
Mortgage type	Fixed 8.5%	
Years	30	
Down payment		15,930

(continued on next page)

ITEM	DATA	AMOUNT
PAYMENT AMOUNT (PER MONTH)		
Mortgage	1,053.41	
Taxes	400	
Total	1,453.41	
Mortgage Application Fee		250
Points (each point=1% of amount borrowed)		
Bank attorney's fee		500
Buyer's attorney's fee		750
Mortgage tax (5% of the mortgage amount)		625
PMI (Private Mortgage Insurance) required if borrowing more than 80% of value		
Homeowner's insurance (fire, hazard, liability)		375
Title insurance		1,116
Tax escrow and pro-rated taxes		4,800

(continued on next page)

ITEM	DATA	AMOUNT
Plot plan and survey		750
Filing fees (mortgage and deed)		75
Fuel adjustments		500
Escrow setup charge		125
Prepaid interest (covers interest until first mortgage payment)		500
Structural tests		225
Pest inspection		60
Water inspection		50
ESTIMATED CLOSING COST		**$10,616**
CASH DOWN PAYMENT		**15,930**
TOTAL CASH NEEDED PURCHASE		**26,546**

"Sue and Dan were confident that they could manage the mortgage, but were a little concerned about their amount of available cash. We discussed the possibility of seller concessions with them—including some of the cash requirements in the sale price. We added the following to the estimate:

$6,372 Seller's concession
$20,174 Actual cash needed for purchase

"Sue and Dan made an offer.

"The seller, knowing that Sue and Dan were well into the process of preapproval, that their credit had been checked, and that they understood and were ready to meet the cash requirements—in other words, that Sue and Dan were serious buyers, and that the sale was likely to go through smoothly—accepted the offer. Negotiations were now complete, subject to testing and contract review of negotiations.

"Sue and Dan had an average waiting period. Testing was completed within ten days, and during that time the seller's attorney drew up a contract, and Sue and Dan submitted full applications and fees to the bank.

"After legal work—title search, and so forth—has been submitted to the bank, and Sue and Dan's mortgage is approved, they're ready to go to closing. The last step—and it's an important one—is the preclosing walk-through, where Sue and Dan are able to verify that the house is still in the condition it was when they agreed to buy it."

I've added a few items to the consolidation worksheet—and I've taken Sue and Dan back in time a little, to before they bought their house, to show how the planning for a major purchase fits into this structure.

The worksheet has been augmented with a "Now" column, and a "Years to planned birth" row, because when you start making financial plans for key events in your life, you need to know how far out in the future these events are going to take place. Don't forget, with the consolidation worksheet/time line format, one of the adjustments you can make is to postpone having a child—and the nice thing about this method is, you don't have to postpone indefinitely. You can make a timetable when you'll be ready.

In this worksheet, Sue and Dan have started to fill in their shelter expenses, to get a more complete picture of what their finances will look like when their babies are born. They're also filling in an estimated income line, and a net income line (after taxes) so that they can gauge their expenses against income—and they're still holding their head above water there, although of course there's more to come.

They've planned their next major expense—buying a house—for three years in the future, between the two babies, and that expense will come from savings. They'll work it through in more detail in the next chapter, when we move from the consolidation worksheet/time line format to a strictly time line format.

Sue and Dan Consolidation Worksheet 3

	Now	Child #1	Child #2	Child #3	Child #4
Years to planned birth		2	4		
Expenses					
Medical (no complications)		$7,800	$7,800		
Medical (fertility treatments)					
Adoption expenses					
Objects (baby clothes, furniture, etc.)		3,985	2,265		
Total baby expenses		11,785	10,065		
Shelter (continuing cost)	30,000	30,000	23,000		
Total current expenses	25,000	25,000	45,000		

(continued on next page)

	Now	Child #1	Child #2	Child #3	Child #4
Total expenses	55,000	66,785	78,065		
Income	120,000	126,000	138,000		
Estimated taxes	46,800	49,140	53,820		
Net income	73,200	76,860	84,180		
Savings to date	15,000				
Projected savings per year	18,200				
Years to planned move	3				
Cash requirement from savings— Down payment on house	21,000				

Here, in the following time line, Sue and Dan are taking those consolidated figures and plugging them into a chronology. They're also starting to fill in their savings lines. They get their "Savings per year" for a given year by subtracting their total expenses from their total (net) income; if they spend more than they make in a given year, it will mean a negative net savings figure—a drawing down on their savings. "Savings to date" is the amount of savings they have brought into that year. If they make a major cash outlay from savings, as Sue and Dan plan to do in 1998 when they buy their house, that is entered as "Cash outlay from savings." Then those three entries—savings per year, savings to date, and cash outlay

from savings—are totaled together to give them that year's
"Net savings."

Sue and Dan Time Line 3

	1996	1997	1998	1999	2000	2001
Total current expenses	$25,000	$25,000	$30,000	$45,000	$50,000	
Total baby expenses		11,785		10,065		
Total shelter expenses (ongoing)	30,000	30,000	30,000	23,000	23,000	
TOTAL EXPENSES	55,000	66,785	60,000	78,065	73,000	
TOTAL (NET) INCOME	**73,200**	**76,860**	**76,860**	**84,180**	**84,180**	
Savings per year	18,200	10,075	16,860	6,115	11,180	
SAVINGS TO DATE	**15,000**	**33,200**	**43,275**	**22,275**	**28,390**	
Cash outlay from savings			21,000			
NET SAVINGS	**33,200**	**43,275**	**22,275**	**28,390**	**39,570**	

5

Child Care—The Most Important Business Relationship You'll Ever Have

Adults need to have some kind of life beyond parenthood, and some adults need more than others. But babies and young children don't take that into account. They need to be cared for all the time, and someone has to do it.

Even if you just plan to go out to a movie once a month, you'll need a baby-sitter. If you plan to work outside the home, you'll be making a major investment—financial and emotional—in child care. And you don't want to overlook either side of that equation.

Turning a part of your child's life over to someone else is the single most important business contract you'll ever negotiate, and it should be treated with at least the same amount of care and attention you'd give to buying a house or making a career change. However, as with any business deal, you have to look at this one realistically. Child care is always a compromise—of child care you want and the child care you can afford. But with some planning and foresight, you can make it the very best compromise possible.

How Much Child Care Do You Need—And How Much Can You Afford?

Should I be going out to work?

If you're a single parent, this question probably answers itself. You do what you have to do.

If you're a couple, and both of you are really committed to a career outside the home, then you know what you want to do, and it's not really an economic decision (although you'll still have to decide what kind of child care you can afford).

But if one of you does not have a strong commitment to a career, and your decision to go back to work is based on "Well, we probably need the money," then before you make the decision to work or not to work, you should ask yourself these questions:

What is a net salary that would make my work out of the home worthwhile?

There are two ways of figuring this. First, what is the total income you need to balance your budget (clear-eyed, realistic, not extravagant)? How do you stand in relation to it? If you're short on funds, how much of a dent will your second-partner net income make?

Second, a good, general rule of thumb: The supplementary income should increase your total household income (net after taxes) by enough to cover current and future expenses over the next ten years.

What kind of child care do I want?

NOTE: You don't frame the question this way if you're a single parent, or if you've definitely made a commitment to both partners working outside the home. Then it's, What kind of child care can I afford?

Read over the different child care options in this chapter, and do more research on them, find out their availability in your area and the rate scale for the options you favor. If work/child care is an option for you and not a necessity, then the number you're using to figure out your net income should reflect the child care option you *really* want, including all its hidden costs. And don't forget the Aggravation Factor. Will finding—and keeping—the right nanny end up being more of a problem than taking care of the kids yourself, with the help of an occasional baby-sitter?

If you're going to be leaving the home to work, you should be considering a live-in or live-out nanny, or a day-care center. And don't forget you have to take your *entire* work schedule into consideration. Will you be working late some nights; will you be traveling for work?

If you're not going to be working full-time, then depending on how much child care you need, you may want to consider day care, an au pair, a baby-sitting service, neighborhood baby-sitters, or a neighborhood co-op arrangement.

What can I deduct?

Check with your accountant, because these rules, like all IRS rules, are subject to bewildering change without notice. Roughly, this is the story:

Your caregiver must be at least 19 years old and cannot be someone you could claim as a dependent. You can (this is new as of 1993, and may be changed again, as with any deduction) deduct for child care if only one parent is working, but at least one parent must be either working or looking for work. You may take a tax credit based on earned income: a percentage of $2,400 per child to a maximum of $4,800. In practice, this is normally 20 percent, or $480 per child. You must fill out a Form 2441 or its successor to receive credit for child care.

What Kinds of Child Care Are There?

NANNIES

What do they do?

A nanny is a full-time employee whose job is taking care of your child or children, including all child-related chores, and *nothing else*. That means seeing that the children's toys are picked up, doing their laundry, fixing snacks and light meals for them. If you expect anything more than that, make sure you advertise for a "nanny/light housework," and make sure that exactly what you mean by "light housework" is spelled out in advance. Notice that even with our basic description of a nanny's chores, there's room for misunderstanding. What is a "light meal"?

In real life, what nannies sometimes do is leave suddenly, feel exploited, or leave you feeling exploited, and the clearer the original agreement is, the better chance you have of avoiding these unfortunate circumstances. A nanny is going to be working very closely with you in a one-to-one employer-employee relationship. This work situation is always going to be dynamic and subject to fluctuation and ongoing renegotiation, which means that it is also always going to be a fertile ground for misunderstanding. Your best bet is to draw up a work contract that covers every foreseeable contingency—the number of children, their ages and specific schedules, the availability and compensation of the nanny for overtime, whether or not you'll allow the nanny to have visitors in your house, etc. (See worksheet below titled Work Contract.)

For what ages are nannies appropriate?

A nanny should be qualified to deal with infants as well as children. You can also hire a *doula,* a specialist in caring for new mothers and newborn infants, as soon as you get home from the hospital.

After your youngest has started school, you might start wondering if you can really justify the expense of someone whose only job is to stay home and take care of children who aren't there. But the answer may still be yes, especially if you're very busy in a high-pressure job or a job that involves traveling. Someone still has to take the kids to the dentist and soccer practice. Your nanny then becomes not so much a nurturer as a driver, meal maker, etc. These changes, of course, will be covered in your regular contract updates.

How do you find a nanny?

There are something like 800 nanny agencies in the United States, and since they're not regulated, you should find out as much as you can about the agency before you proceed with it.

Word-of-mouth, personal testimonials are always useful—if you don't know anyone who has gotten a nanny through a particular service before, ask the service for a list of families who have used it. Ask the service to explain its screening process to you, and check the credentials and references of the nannies it recommends.

Nanny services can be found through family and parenting magazines, and also through regional magazines like *The Washingtonian* in Washington, D.C., which periodically publish articles on finding nannies in a given area. The National Association for Childcare and Resource and Referral Agencies in Rochester, Minnesota, (507) 287-2020, has lists of local agencies in all parts of the country.

What credentials should a nanny have?

There is no formal certification for nannies in the United States (there is in England). There are reputable "nanny schools," and it counts for something if your nanny has completed a course of study at one of them, but it is not a real degree or board certification. These schools typically have a twelve- to nineteen-week course of study. Many community colleges offer one-year child care programs or two-year associate degrees. A Red Cross course in CPR and emergency care is a handy thing for your nanny to have, so is a valid driver's license if you want her/him to drive your child anywhere. References from former employers should be carefully scrutinized—and followed up with calls to the writers of those references. The worksheet below "Nanny Credentials" will give you a checklist of things you may want to require from a nanny.

Since a nanny is going to be working with you and your children, a face-to-face meeting is the best test—with both you and your children. This isn't always possible. Sometimes if you're hiring through an agency, you'll be hiring a nanny from out of town. In these cases, you should at least arrange for an extended telephone interview—and make sure you know the agency's policy for dealing with an obvious mismatch. What happens if, within the first few days, either you or the nanny decides it's not going to work out? Is there a refund of the agency's referral fee, a free replacement, or both?

CHECKING OUT YOUR NANNY

Don't forget: being a nanny is not the most prestigious job in America, nor is it likely to be a fast career track. So the person who has the most qualifications on paper is not always going to be the best qualified for the job. Why does that M.A. in Child Development want to move into your house and take care of your three-year-old?

Anyone who decides to become a nanny has a story behind his/her career choice, and while that story isn't likely to be *The Hand That Rocks the Cradle*, anyone who's ever hired a nanny is likely to have had at least one or two really strange experiences, so it's still in your best interests to find out what your job applicant's story is. No personal interview is going to uncover everything, but try to probe as thoroughly as you can in these areas: What are you expecting from this job? What made you decide to get into this line of work?

The young woman from Wyoming may be looking for a few years of work while she puts herself through college at night; she may be looking for an environment where she's not the only person who's heard of James Joyce; or she may be escaping a violent marriage or an abusive family. The practical nurse/nutritionist/child psychologist may be working off the books for a family because she's an illegal alien (and this can be true if she's a Mary Poppins look-alike with an upper-crust British accent, just as easily as if she's from Latin America or the Philippines). The sweet grandparent can be looking for an outlet for her maternal instincts or a place to do some private drinking. Anyone who wants to work (and perhaps live) in someone else's home may not so much be looking to care for your child as to be taken care of.

A man can make just as good a nanny as a woman, and we aren't using any gender-specific language in talking about caregivers here, but there aren't many men in this field, and if you get a male applicant, once again you'd be well advised to find out why he's decided to become a nanny.

If you want to find out more about your prospective nanny's background, here are some tips:

You can check out all the checkable items on the résumé. Call her/his previous landlord, and find out what kind of tenant she/he was. Put this information in perspective—landlords can be vindictive, too.

You can contact the police department of the town where your prospective nanny last lived. You can't ask for a rap sheet, but you can ask if they know any reason why this person should not be hired as a nanny.

Actually, you already have at your disposal one of the best private investigative forces you could hire—your insurance company. Put your nanny on your car insurance policy as a driver, and they'll check out every blemish in every state on his/her driving.

If you add your nanny to your homeowners liability policy,

it's almost as good as getting her/him bonded. Before the insurance company will extend coverage to this new person, they'll do a complete background check, including police record and credit rating.

A new organization, The Childcare Registry, has recently been developed to help address this problem. TCR president, Ellen Tauscher, started the computerized database network "after many years of observing the underlying fear and uncertainty instilled in my friends and family when they were looking for someone responsible to care for their children. . . . For example, my friends always wondered if their child care provider had an impaired driving record, since they were responsible for driving the children from place to place on a daily basis." The Childcare Registry, headquartered in San Francisco (800-CCR-0033), provides a verification of date of birth, Social Security number, and such issues as employment status, driving record, criminal and civil judgments, and educational degree verification.

What about making it legal?

If you hire anyone who makes more than $50 a quarter, the government requires you to declare it. This is a sufficiently expensive and difficult process that the IRS estimates, conservatively, that 75 percent of all Americans who hire household help do not pay Social Security taxes. Nevertheless, the laws are on the books, and they call for fines and even imprisonment as penalties for breaking them. Oh yes, you can also forget about running for public office.

There are other pitfalls. Illegal household helpers, paid subminimum wages off the books, have been known to sue their employers and win. And if you're going to hire a nanny off the books, *make absolutely certain you sit down with your insurance agent and find out what you're covered for and what you're not covered for.*

To make certain you're completely legal, check the third worksheet in this chapter, "The Legal Household Helper."

Sponsoring an alien worker for a green card is technically possible, but it's extremely difficult, and at best is a process that can take years.

What can you expect to pay?

This varies greatly depending on the part of the country you live in, the experience of the nanny, the number of children in the household, the duties contracted for, whether or not the nanny lives in, and a variety of other factors (including the legality of the contract). You can expect to pay from $175 to $450 a week for a nanny, although they can come cheaper or more expensive. And don't forget, if a nanny is going to be with you for any length of time, she/he will expect periodic raises, either yearly or twice-yearly. The average raise is 5 to 7 percent of the nanny's weekly salary.

If you hire a nanny through an agency, you'll have to pay the agency a referral fee, typically no more than one to three months of their salary.

For a legally contracted nanny, you'll have to pay Social Security—and, in some states, unemployment insurance and workmen's compensation.

What "hidden costs" are there in hiring a nanny?

Sit down with your insurance agent before you hire a nanny and discuss any changes that have to be made in your coverage—if the nanny is living in, if she/he will be driving your car. etc.

If your nanny is from a different part of the country (or world), what travel costs will you have to pay? See the worksheet "The Legal Household Helper," which lists all the expenses you'll incur to square yourself with the government.

Nanny Work Contract

These are some of the important categories that should be included in a work contract. Use this as a guideline to make up your own contract, making sure you cover everything of importance for your own particular household. Don't expect that you're really going to be able to think of everything in advance—that's why it's important to make sure the contract includes a regular schedule for review and renegotiation.

- ❏ Salary
  - ❏ How much?
  - ❏ When paid?
  - ❏ What is deducted?
  - ❏ Paid in cash or check?
  - ❏ Schedule of raises
- ❏ Duties
  - ❏ Meals
    - ❏ Food shopping—You make list or nanny does?
    - ❏ How prepared (for example, organic foods, make own baby food)
  - ❏ Housework (specify frequency)
    - ❏ Change sheets
    - ❏ Laundry
    - ❏ Dusting
    - ❏ Any duties not connected with children
  - ❏ What to do with children
    - ❏ Indoor/outdoor Play
    - ❏ Read
    - ❏ Lessons
    - ❏ TV or no TV
  - ❏ Other
    - ❏ Care for pets?
    - ❏ Responsibility for children's friends—sleepover, etc.
- ❏ Driving
  - ❏ Regular driving duties with children
  - ❏ May/may not use car for personal use
  - ❏ Who pays for gas if car is used for personal errands?
- ❏ Review of performance
  - ❏ Chain of command—who does nanny answer to?
  - ❏ Schedule of performance review
  - ❏ Schedule of contract review

❏ Work Schedule
   ❏   Hours
   ❏   Days off
   ❏   How much flexibility in schedule (yours/nanny's)?
❏ Time off
   ❏   How many weeks vacation?
   ❏   What is paid?
❏ Provision for emergency leave
❏ Privileges
   ❏   Smoke?
   ❏   Entertain guests in home?
   ❏   TV in room?
❏ Infant care, health and safety
   ❏   Creative play
   ❏   Family structure and dynamics
❏ Nanny's expenses—who pays for:
   ❏   Sundry items?
   ❏   Food for special diet?
   ❏   Emergency leave?
   ❏   Nanny's extra expenses on family vacation?

A couple more tips: Make sure you find out how long your nanny wants the job for. If this is just a short-term thing for her/him, but he/she meets your requirements better than anyone else does, you may want to make the deal anyway—but at least you won't be letting yourself in for an unpleasant surprise. There's nothing more frustrating than finding Mary Poppins incarnate, spending months teaching her your routine so that she fits perfectly into your household, then discovering that she plans to leave for college in the fall.

Another thing to make sure you've spelled out, with the i's dotted and the t's crossed: What's a five-day week for a live-in nanny? If your nanny plans to take weekends off, you'll want to define exactly what that means. It's a good idea to write into the contract that the work week starts on Sunday night. That way, if there are problems or special instructions, you'll have time to go over them. The alternative is a note, which can be misunderstood, or over-the-shoulder instructions called out as you're flying out the door . . . which can certainly be misunderstood.

You'll want a clear understanding about Friday evenings as well. You may not be able to get your nanny to agree to a clause that says your Friday night plans take precedence over hers anytime, but you can try to negotiate an agreement that covers you for, say, those times when you're traveling on business and your Friday return flight is delayed.

Always have a local fill-in baby-sitter you can call for nights off and emergencies.

Nanny Credentials

❏ Identification
   ❏ Driver's license
   ❏ Social Security number
   ❏ Passport
❏ Driving skills
   ❏ Clean license
   ❏ Owns car
   ❏ Past accident record
❏ Communication skills
   ❏ Speaks English
   ❏ Can read and write in English
   ❏ Speaks a foreign language
❏ First aid skills
   ❏ Red Cross nursing course
   ❏ CPR course
❏ College or other courses in:
   ❏ Child development
   ❏ Child nutrition
   ❏ Infant care, health, and safety
   ❏ Creative play
   ❏ Family structure and dynamics
❏ Certificate of health from a physician
❏ Letters of reference
❏ School transcripts
❏ Insurance

❑ Other history of working with children
   ❑ Previous nanny jobs
   ❑ Experience with children not related to nanny
   ❑ Experience with children related to nanny
   ❑ Has children
   ❑ Younger siblings
❑ Other special skills
   ❑ Plays an instrument
   ❑ Sews or knits
   ❑ Athletic/coaching experience
   ❑ Other
❑ Reasons for choosing profession
❑ Future plans—expects to stay how long?

THE LEGAL HOUSEHOLD HELPER

When do you need to file?

Any time you're employing someone you pay over $50 a quarter. The exception to this—and it's tricky—is an *independent contractor,* someone who supplies her/his own tools and does the same work for a number of different people. Obviously, this is not likely to apply to a nanny—it may to a baby-sitter. If you're not sure which category someone falls under, and you care enough—for example, if you're expecting to be Attorney General of the United States—check with an attorney.

You're required to file, and pay Social Security taxes, even if your employee is an illegal alien.

How do you do it?

Get an employer ID number from the Internal Revenue Service.

Make payments quarterly.

Pay 15.3 percent of employee's gross income as Social Security tax.

If you pay an employee more than $1,000 per quarter, you must pay federal unemployment tax of up to $56 per year.

Check with your state tax office for disability and work-men's compensation payments (most are due quarterly).

If you withhold income taxes for your nanny, these payments are also due quarterly.

DAY-CARE CENTERS

What do they do?

Day-care centers are operated out of people's homes or out of specifically designated institutions. They offer pretty much what they say they do—care during the day for a group of children. Beyond that, they can vary widely—in the physical setup of the facility, the number and age range of children they take in at one time, and the amount of supervision. Since there are such wide differences between different facilities, it's essential that you visit a facility you're considering and find out exactly what they do offer.

For what ages is day care appropriate?

If you're considering day care, you'll start to need it at whatever point you need to go back to work. Unlike nannies, who are individual contractors and who'll expect to start working within a very short time after they've been contracted to work, day-care centers are always there, so you can start visiting centers in your neighborhood, and deciding what you want for your child, even before the baby is born. In fact, this is probably a good idea. Good day-care centers can fill up, so it can be important to get your child on the waiting list. For a complete checklist of questions to ask about day care, see the worksheet in the chapter called "Day Care Questions."

What's the difference between licensed and unlicensed home day-care centers?

To get a license, the caregiver's home must pass a background check, and her/his home must pass certain health and safety standards. These vary from state to state, but in general, they run along these lines:

For the caregiver—and all other adults in the household: A clean bill of health from a physician (and from a vet, if there are pets in the house). A background check of possible police records, history of mental illness, history of child abuse in the family.

For the premises: Safety precautions, including fire exits, smoke alarms, fenced-in play areas, a controlled temperature. House in good repair, adequate bathroom facilities for the number of children being cared for.

For the facility: A maximum allowable number of children, which may vary according to the ages of the children.

Licensed day-care practitioners usually charge more than unlicensed caregivers. (Since these rates vary so widely in different parts of the country, it's impossible to give even a ball-park estimate of what you can expect to pay.) Licensed practitioners can get a homeowners insurance policy that covers the children in their care, which unlicensed caregivers cannot. They are also required to take referrals from the state or county—children of welfare parents.

Here again, the most important consideration is: Are you happy with the caregiver and the environment? Is your child happy? Many unlicensed centers are wonderful, the caregivers loving responsible parents whose homes fail to meet some particular of the local code. However, if you use one, it's a good idea to check out your own insurance coverage.

Finally, if you're looking at a family home day-care center, find out what sort of backup the caregiver has. If she/he gets sick, will you suddenly have to make other arrangements for your child on short notice?

CHILD CARE CENTERS

Child care centers are typically located in schools, churches, community rec centers, or municipal buildings, or (rarely) within the parent's place of employment.

If your employer provides a day-care center, you're home free. Well, no one with kids is ever home free. You still have to worry about what to do if you travel, or if you have to work late at the office past the company's day-care hours, or what to do if your child gets sick, or if you have a baby who's too young for the program. . . .

Still, if you're planning a family, and either parent has a chance to switch jobs to a company that does provide good, subsidized or affordable day care, that should certainly be a consideration in your career decision.

A child care center may be more reliable than a family home in that it will have a larger staff, so that you won't have to worry about your caregiver getting sick or canceling out on you. On the other hand, it may be understaffed. It's likely to be more expensive than a family home—here again, you have to shop around—and, of course, there may not be one convenient to you. You can expect it to meet safety standards, and be properly insured—although here again, no bureaucracy is a substitute for your own judgment. If the place looks as if it's not well maintained, then it's probably not.

Here's a checklist for evaluating day-care providers, adapted from recommendations by the New York State Department of Social Services. These are the evaluations you should make on visiting the center.

Day Care Questions: The Care Providers

	YES	NO
Is the center licensed? Is the license current?		
Are there enough adults for the number and age of children?*		
Are the children encouraged to make friends with other children? Are they happy and playing with each other?		
Are the caregivers sensitive to the children? Do they recognize when a child is upset or excited, and deal with it?		

*Here's what the New York State Department of Social Services recommends:

AGE OF CHILD	NUMBER OF CHILDREN PER ADULT
8 weeks–1.5 years	4
1.5–3 years	5
3 years	7
4 years	8
5 years	9
6–10 years	10
10–14 years	15

Health and Safety

	YES	No
Are there sanitary facilities for diapering activities?		
Is the place well lit and ventilated, and free of hazards? (Radiators covered, stairways and windows protected, safety caps on electrical outlets, walkways free of ice and snow, outdoor space fenced and clean)		
Are heavy pieces of furniture stable so that they can't tip over?		
Are medicines and hazardous materials locked up?		
Are there smoke detectors and fire extinguishers?		
Are toys and equipment clean and in good repair?		
Do caregivers get annual health examinations?		
Is there a written health record kept for each child?		
Are there written procedures for securing background checks on new caregivers?		
Are first aid supplies available?		

(continued on next page)

	YES	No
Does a registered nurse visit at least weekly in programs for children under three years old?		
Are there written procedures for reporting suspected cases of abuse or neglect?		
Is there an adult responsible for receiving children when they arrive each day?		
Can the facility assure you that your child will not be released to anyone else without your written permission?		
Are there written procedures to follow when a child gets sick?		
Does the caregiver provide healthy and attractive meals, prepared and served in a clean space?		
Are there arrangements made for children on special diets?		
Does at least one caregiver have current Red Cross first aid certification?		

Environment

	YES	No
Do the caregivers respect the children's rights to play alone or with others?		
Is the space arranged so that children can select materials according to their own interests and abilities, and return them when they've finished?		
Do the caregivers praise the children and encourage their self-confidence?		
Is the program well equipped with supplies such as blocks, books, games, toys, and creative art materials?		
Is there limited access to television?		
Is there space for active play and quiet play?		
Is there a place for each child's personal belongings?		
Is there a special place for a sick child to rest and yet allow the caregiver to give him/her attention?		
Can children reach the toilet and sink easily and safely?		

Arrangements

	YES	No
Did the caregiver adequately explain the program to you?		
Will the caregiver provide you with regular updates on your child's activities and progress?		
Were you encouraged to visit and observe the program at any time?		
Is the daily schedule available to parents?		
Will field trips be adequately supervised? Will your written permission be obtained for each trip?		

Fees and Scheduling

How much is the fee per child? For more than one child?	
How often is payment made?	
What's the payment policy when a child is absent due to sickness or other causes?	
When can I bring my children? When must they be picked up? Is there any flexibility in this schedule?	
What arrangements are made for notifying parents about sick children?	

Answers here are more detailed than yes or no.

BABY-SITTERS

A baby-sitting arrangement is likely to be a more sporadic one. However, if you use the same baby-sitter regularly, on a regular schedule, you should make sure that you're legal, under the definitions outlined above.

When you're interviewing a prospective baby-sitter, it's important to make sure she's mature enough, and resourceful enough, to handle being left in charge of your children, and your house, while you're away. Here's a checklist of things you can do when selecting a baby-sitter.

Ask for references. Of course, this isn't always possible. Baby-sitting is generally an entry level job into the world of work, and you may be your young prospective employee's first client. Don't rule out a first-time baby-sitter—especially if she lives nearby and you know her family—but in this field, like so many others, it's nice to have someone who's experienced.

Ask how she'd handle emergencies. You can't absolutely count on a young person keeping her head in an emergency, but you're going to feel safer with someone who's given some thought to it and has a plan.

Here are some questions you might ask:

What would you do if you smelled smoke? The prospective baby-sitter should want to make sure she knows where all the exits from the house are, and what your plan of evacuation is (you'll walk her through all this). She should know that the first things she needs to do is to get the children safely out of the house, then go to a neighbor and have them call the fire department.

What would you do if the child started to choke? It's wonderful if you have a baby-sitter who knows the Heimlich maneuver, but you can't count on this. You do need to have a baby-sitter who won't panic, who'll do what she can. Holding the child upside down can work for mild choking episodes—

what's really important here is, when you start discussing these emergency situations, that you don't have a baby-sitter who'll wrinkle her nose and say, "Ewwww, gross—I don't want to think about those things."

Who would you call/where would you go in an emergency? You should have emergency phone numbers next to your phone, or on your speed dial (don't trust the speed dial alone—have the numbers written down, too). The baby-sitter should know exactly where they are. He or she should know how to reach his or her parents, or your neighbors.

He or she should also know where the local hospital or emergency treatment center is, and how to get there. And you have to make sure that the hospital will admit your child if she's not accompanied by a legal guardian. This actually happened to me. Kyle was with her nanny when she had a choking fit. The nanny rushed her to the hospital, where she was told that they couldn't admit a child who wasn't with a legal guardian or family member.

Yes, that's what they said. And no, I don't know what they could possibly have been thinking. Yes, I do. They were thinking, how can we be sure we're going to get paid and not sued? I know what they weren't thinking, and that's: *Here's a child in trouble. What can we do?* I only know how lucky I was to have a nanny who wouldn't accept it. She asked, "Where are the doctors?"

"They're back there in the examining rooms, and you can't . . . "

But she did. She took Kyle in her arms, pushed past the nurse at the desk, went back into the examining rooms and grabbed the first doctor she saw by the stethoscope, and demanded, "Do you have children? Then take care of this child."

What do you do if the child can't sleep? You want someone who'll read to the child, stay with her, calm her fears if she's afraid.

Working Child Care into Your Budget

Child care expenses are among the most widely variable expenses you'll confront, from nothing (if one of you stays home, and you have grandma to baby-sit) to a major expense. Here again, the best way to approach figuring them out is to start with your ideal scenario and scale back if necessary.

How Much Child Care Do You Need?

HOW MUCH TIME CAN YOU SPEND WITH CHILD?		AGE OF CHILD			
		BIRTH–3	3–5	SCHOOL AGE	HIGH SCHOOL
Can spend full-time at home	Parent 1				
	Parent 2				
Can spend part-time at home	Parent 1				
	Parent 2				
Working full-time	Parent 1				
	Parent 2				

If you're just starting out, planning for children in the future, this will be real guesswork, but it will give you an idea of the kind of budget you'll need to plan . . . or perhaps revise, as time goes on.

The first of these worksheets is for child care that will cover all of your children—for example, you'll only need one nanny, even if you have three kids. The second is for child care options that will entail a separate expense for each child. So you'll need to fill out as many versions of this worksheet as you have children.

Child Care Costs (All Children)

IDEAL CHILD CARE SITUATION	EXPENSE	YEARS UNTIL EXPENSE	YEARS OF EXPENSE
Nanny			
Au pair			
Co-op			
Occasional baby-sitter			

Child Care Costs (Each Child)

IDEAL CHILD CARE SITUATION	EXPENSE	YEARS UNTIL EXPENSE	YEARS OF EXPENSE
Preschool			
Day-care			
After-school care			

In order to place these figures in the time line, you'll need to know not only how much your child care of choice will cost, but at what point in your financial future it will start, and for how long it will last.

At this point, as you move beyond childbirth and home-buying expenses, the rest of your expenses become time-oriented, so the consolidation worksheets become no longer necessary. If you have more children, or decide to buy another house, you'd figure them into a new consolidation worksheet. But from here on in, you'll be using the time line as the principle tool for your financial plan.

	1996	1997	1998	1999	2000	2001	2002	2003	2004
Total current expenses									
Total baby expenses									
Total child care expenses									
Total shelter expenses (ongoing)									
TOTAL EXPENSES									
TOTAL (NET) INCOME									
Savings rate									
SAVINGS TO DATE									
Cash outlay from savings									
NET SAVINGS									

Sue and Dan

Sue and Dan planned to get a nanny to take care of their children while Sue commuted to New York and Dan worked at building up a new business. Here's how they began plugging in their figures. To be thorough, they researched both a nanny and day care.

Sue and Dan: Child Care Costs (Two Children)

IDEAL CHILD CARE SITUATION	EXPENSE	YEARS UNTIL EXPENSE	YEARS OF EXPENSE
Nanny	$25,000	2	7
Au pair			
Co-op			
Occasional baby-sitter	500	2	14

Sue and Dan: Child 1 (First Child)

IDEAL CHILD CARE SITUATION	EXPENSE	YEARS UNTIL EXPENSE	YEARS OF EXPENSE
Preschool	1,200	6	2
Day care	4,800	2	3
After-school care			

Sue and Dan: Child 2 (Second Child)

IDEAL CHILD CARE SITUATION	EXPENSE	YEARS UNTIL EXPENSE	YEARS OF EXPENSE
Preschool	1,200	8	2
Day care	4,800	4	3
After-school care			

Because child care is an expense that will start with the birth of their first child and continue for the next several years, Sue and Dan have to start projecting their time line farther out:

Sue and Dan Time Line 4a

	1996	1997	1998	1999
Total current expenses	$25,000	$25,000	$30,000	$45,000
Total baby expenses		11,785		10,065
Total child care expenses		25,500	25,500	25,500
Total shelter expenses (ongoing)	30,000	30,000	30,000	23,000
TOTAL EXPENSES	55,000	92,285	85,500	103,565
TOTAL (NET) INCOME	**73,200**	**76,860**	**76,860**	**84,180**
Savings per year	18,200	<15,425>	<8,640>	
SAVINGS TO DATE	**15,000**	**33,200**	**18,275**	
Cash outlay from savings			21,000	
NET SAVINGS	**33,200**	**17,775**	**<11,365>**	

Sue and Dan are coming face to face with some realities here—their dream scenario is going to have to be revised. If they stick to their plans to have a full-time nanny, they aren't going to be able to afford to buy their house.

They have to revise their plans for either housing or child care. They go back over their time line, and plug in the figures they have projected for day care. Their budget becomes manageable again:

2000	2001	2002	2003	2004
$50,000	$50,000	$50,000	$50,000	$50,000
25,500	26,200	26,200	26,200	26,200
23,000	23,000	23,000	23,000	23,000
98,500	99,700	99,700	99,700	99,700
84,180	**84,180**	**84,180**	**84,180**	**84,180**

Sue and Dan Time Line 4b

	1996	1997	1998	1999
Total current expenses	$25,000	$25,000	$30,000	$45,000
Total baby expenses		11,785		10,065
Total child care expenses			5,300	5,300
Total shelter expenses (ongoing)	30,000	30,000	30,000	23,000
TOTAL EXPENSES	55,000	66,800	65,300	83,400
TOTAL (NET) INCOME	**73,200**	**76,860**	**76,860**	**84,180**
Savings per year	18,200	10,060	11,560	780
SAVINGS TO DATE	**15,000**	**33,200**	**43,260**	**33,820**
Cash outlay from savings			21,000	
NET SAVINGS	**33,200**	**43,260**	**33,820**	**34,600**

2000	2001	2002	2003	2004
$50,000	$50,000	$50,000	$50,000	$50,000
10,100	6,500	6,500	1,700	1,700
23,000	23,000	23,000	23,000	23,000
83,100	79,500	79,500	74,700	74,700
84,180	**84,180**	**84,180**	**84,180**	**84,180**
1,080	4,680	4,680	9,680	9,680
34,600				
35,680				

6

Thinking About College

From day care to college? Well, it is true it that feels as though our children grow up before we know it. As the old song goes, "Turn around, and you're ten . . . turn around, and you're grown"—but it doesn't really happen quite that fast. What does happen right away is this: You have to start thinking about college almost as soon as you start having children.

College is the culmination of your children's time as full-time dependents, and it's your biggest single expense for them as well. In planning for your kids' college, you need to start early, and you need to plan on three different levels:

First, how much is your kids' college going to cost you? This breaks down into two different subcategories. Make sure you know the range of possible cost between the most expensive private colleges, plus graduate or professional school, and the least expensive state colleges. Then, make sure you know what *all* the expenses of college will be—tuition is only the beginning of it.

Second, how can you set up a savings or investment plan to build a nest egg that will be ready and waiting for your kids when they get to college?

Third, how much can you reduce that cost? This means

finding out about scholarships—what scholarships are available for your child, and which ones he/she can get. It means finding out about loans, and it means finding out about reducing the tuition itself, by such methods as advanced placement courses so that your child can finish a semester, or even a year, earlier.

Finally, how much of this expense are you going to take responsibility for? I feel very strongly about this, and I know it can work: *Parents should pay for 75 percent of their children's college education.* The child should be responsible for the other 25 percent. There are various ways she can do this, and we'll discuss them later in the chapter. I believe, also, that parents' obligation to their children's education lasts for the four years of college, and no further. After that, the child is on his own. It's certainly appropriate, if you want to and can afford it, to make a loan to a child for graduate or professional school, but it should be just that, a loan, with a note drawn up stipulating repayment terms and interest.

How Much Is College Going to Cost You?

I've said before that you have to reevaluate your options and priorities regularly. Nowhere is this truer than in your college planning, because college planning (a) involves big numbers, and (b) is best done a long time in advance. That means there is plenty of room for your goals to shift, and time to readjust if they do start shifting.

How much is college going to cost you? These are my best estimates at the present time. The further out you have to project, the more approximate the estimate. But we do know that during the past decade, college costs have consistently outpaced inflation by about 2 percent per year, and most experts predict that this trend is going to continue—the figure that's commonly used is a 6 percent increase per year.

As you get closer to the date when your child is eligible to start college, make sure the numbers below are still accurate.

But if you have young children, you can start with these figures to create your saving goals.

Here are current figures and projections for some representative colleges around the country, compiled by the Life Insurance Marketing and Research Association, Inc. (LIMRA), in Hartford, Connecticut. The figures for state schools apply to residents of that state only.

Table 3: Estimated College Costs: Four-Year Tuition, Fees, Room and Board

COLLEGE	STUDENT BEGINS COLLEGE IN			
CATEGORY	**1995**	**2000**	**2005**	**2010**
State college	$35,230	$47,184	$70,812	$84,616
Private college, less expensive	$47,510	$63,630	$85,264	$114,109
Private college, medium range	$63,280	$84,750	$113,565	$151,985
Private college, expensive	$105,571	$141,390	$189,462	$253,559

Of course, that's not the whole story. The complete picture of college costs—the ones you can't do without—looks like this:

Tuition and fees: The above projections are approximate, of course—no one really suggests that you can predict down to the last dollar how much a four-year expense is going to be, starting in 2010. But you can use them as a guide to building a savings plan when you start your own worksheet.

Room and board: There are a variety of off-campus housing arrangements that can be cheaper (or more expensive) than dorm life, but we'll use on-campus housing as the benchmark here.

Personal expenses: Includes telephone and cable TV bills, dorm room furnishings your child doesn't have already (he can take his stereo from home), clothing items, grooming items, a budget for entertainment.

Books and supplies: If your child is starting college in 1995, a computer is already pretty much of a necessity. We don't pretend to know what technological needs will be in 2008.

Travel and transportation: This figure has huge possibilities for variation, depending on how far away from home your child goes to school (and how homesick he gets), and depending on how isolated the campus is. Will she need a car? Cab fare? In any case, unless buying a car is involved, this won't be a large part of the expense—but here as elsewhere, it's better to estimate how *much* it might cost you, so that you have the chance to be pleasantly surprised, rather than shocked and dismayed.

When you're using these worksheets to estimate costs in the future, for savings purposes, round off and "guesstimate" these figures. As you get closer to the actual college date, you should be able to put the figures in with much more accuracy.

For the following worksheet, choose the college you're most likely to be using. If you're not sure, your safest bet is probably to choose the most expensive one for the purposes of setting your savings goals.

Estimated College Expenses—Room and Board

ITEM	ESTIMATED $			
	YEAR 1	YEAR 2	YEAR 3	YEAR 4
Dorm housing				
On-campus dining				
TOTAL				
Off-campus rent				
Meals				
TOTAL				
Living at home: room				
Living at home: board				
TOTAL				

Estimated Annual Personal Expenses

ITEM	ESTIMATED $			
	YEAR 1	YEAR 2	YEAR 3	YEAR 4
Telephone bills				
Cable TV bills				
Dorm room furnishings				

(continued on next page)

ITEM	ESTIMATED $			
	YEAR 1	YEAR 2	YEAR 3	YEAR 4
Clothing				
Grooming items				
Entertainment				
Other				
TOTAL				

Annual Books and Supplies

ITEM	ESTIMATED $			
	YEAR 1	YEAR 2	YEAR 3	YEAR 4
Textbooks				
Desk supplies				
Computer				
Computer supplies				
Electronic information services				

(continued on next page)

ITEM	ESTIMATED $			
	YEAR 1	YEAR 2	YEAR 3	YEAR 4
Other				
TOTAL				

Annual Travel and Transportation

ITEM	ESTIMATED $			
	YEAR 1	YEAR 2	YEAR 3	YEAR 4
Plane/train travel to/from school				
Car				
Car upkeep				
Public transportation				
Other				
TOTAL				

Total Projection of College Expenses

Make out one of these for each college you're considering for each child.

Child's Name:			College:			
Year	**Tuition and Fees**	**Personal Expenses**	**Room and Board**	**Living Expenses**	**Travel and Transportation**	**Total**
Total						

From the figures in the last worksheet, you can estimate the amount of money you'll need to save and when you'll need to save it by:

Savings Goal

Child's Name	Years to College	Estimated Total Cost	College Savings to Date	Needed to Save	Savings Per Year

Your Child's Contribution: 25 Percent

Parents always want to do the best they can for their children. But a crucial part of doing the best for your children is giving them the empowerment that comes with taking responsibility.

Here's what I recommend.

Your child should be prepared to take responsibility for one-quarter of his college expenses. He can do this in a number of ways:

First, he should have been saving for college ever since he started making money. I've written and lectured widely about my jar system of budgeting money, but in brief: Out of every dollar your child has earned, out of every gift he's been given since he first started getting an allowance and doing chores, he should have been putting aside one-third in long-term savings, toward his college education.

He can take advanced-placement classes in high school, so that he enters college with credit toward graduation already in hand. NOTE: Make sure this will actually help you at the college of your child's choice. Some schools will allow students to waive introductory courses if they've done well in advanced placement, but still require them to pay for four years of college.

Also, about 150 public and private high schools in the United States offer intensive two-year college preparatory programs leading to an International Baccalaureate (IB). This diploma qualifies a student for as much as a year's worth of credits at approximately 500 colleges and universities. Your child's high school guidance counselor should have information.

He can take a heavier course load in college, so that he graduates in three years. If he's planning to choose this alternative, he must make sure that the college of his choice allows it. It's becoming a more popular option in recent years, but it is still not universally offered.

NOTE: Here's something your children can start doing when they're young, which can make a genuine difference in saving money on college later on. Many colleges offer scholarships for girls who reach the Gold Award in Girl Scouts, or, for boys, the Eagle Scout level in Boy Scouts. If your child is involved in scouting, she could well be making an important investment in her future.

School Aid

Your child may be able to get aid, in the form of scholarship or a grant, a work-study program, or a guaranteed student loan.

A scholarship or grant can come from the college, or from state or federal sources. As we go into the second half of the nineties, a lot of these programs are being eliminated, but they're still worth looking into. If your child is eligible, the funding is there for her education, and neither you nor she has to pay anything back. It's free money—really free, because it's tax-free. This means that if you're in the 40 percent tax bracket, a $2,000 grant is equivalent to receiving $3,334 in pretax income.

A scholarship may be free money, but it's money your child has earned by dint of scholarly, athletic, or other efforts. And a scholarship may have some strings attached. I received a partial academic scholarship to American University in Washington, but I had to maintain a 3.75 average in order to keep it.

If your child scores high on the Scholastic Aptitude Test (SAT), she'll have a better chance at more prestigious colleges and academic scholarships. There are books and prep courses designed to teach students how to improve SAT scores.

Many colleges offer merit scholarships to top students, regardless of financial need.

Here are a couple of good sources of general information on college financial aid: *The A's and B's of Academic Scholarships* (Octameron, $7) and *College Financial Aid* (Arco, $22).

There may be a Federal Work Study (FWS) program available on campus—a government subsidized program that provides part-time jobs to students. The money earned is either put toward tuition or living expenses. I was also on work-study at American; I worked 10 hours a week for a professor and received minimum wage.

In addition to work-study, there are a variety of other university jobs, such as resident hall assistant jobs (which can include free room and board), food service jobs, a variety of jobs with college athletic departments, even security jobs.

For more information on campus money-making opportunities see: *College Checkmate: Innovative Tuition Plans That Make You a Winner* (Octameron, $7).

Of course, a student can find a part-time job off-campus too, but it'll be easier to work class hours around an on-campus work-study job.

You don't want to overload your child with too much of a workload, if at all possible. Most experts say that any more than ten hours will significantly detract from the student's academic college experience,

She can apply for a student loan. These loans are most often subsidized and guaranteed by state or federal governments at rates usually much lower than a regular unsecured loan. Usually, no interest is charged while the student is in school and no repayment is required until the student has graduated or left college.

Of course, this doesn't mean no interest ever. A student who takes out a loan is going to have work out from under a heavy debt when she graduates. Here are a few numbers to give you an idea of what that debt might be. These are based on paying back the loan over ten years, at an interest rate of 8 percent (table from *College Costs 101*, published by the Prudential Insurance Company of America).

Table 4: Loan Repayment Costs

LOAN	MONTHLY PAYMENT	INTEREST CHARGED OVER LIFE OF LOAN	TOTAL REPAYMENT
$10,000	$121	$ 4,559	$14,559
12,500	152	5,699	18,199
25,000	303	11,398	36,398
50,000	607	22,796	72,796

Today, a popular federal student loan program is the unsubsidized variable rate Stafford Loan for $2,625 to $5,500 annually, available to any full- or part-time undergraduate. The amount increases as the student progresses through school. Payments can be deferred until six months after graduation. At that time, your child can choose from a number of options to repay, including one that requires him to pay a fixed percentage of annual income, say 5 percent or 10 percent until the debt is retired (the government pays the interest while he's still in school).

Banks, credit unions, and other private lenders make most Stafford Loans, which are insured by state guarantee agencies and reinsured by the federal government. Applications are available from most banks and college financial aid offices.

NOTE: You might ask financial aid officers for the names of Stafford lenders that sell their loans to the Student Loan Marketing Association (Sallie Mae). The company will knock 2 percentage points off a loan's interest rate after the borrower makes the first 48 monthly payments on time. Graduates who ask Sallie Mae to deduct their monthly payments directly from their bank accounts can get an additional ¼-point discount.

Your child can also cut borrowing costs by spending nine months to a year as a member of Americorps, the federal government's new national service organization. In 1995, some 20,000 volunteers participated in the program, which will be expanded to about 100,000 in 1996. Call (800) 942-2677 for information and an application. In exchange for a living allowance of about $7,500, a participant works for a year in a community service program, such as an environmental task force, and then receives $4,725 for future college tuition or to help pay student loans.

Your application for financial aid, whether it be loans, grants, or scholarships, has a lot better chance of success if you understand the process.

As your kids are working on their admissions applications, you'll need to start gathering your own records.

You'll have to fill out a *Need Analysis Form.* You can get this from your kids' high school guidance office. It's filled out after Jan. 1 of a student's senior year in high school. Check with the college to see which forms they accept—there are different types.

All undergraduate applicants for aid will have to fill out a *Free Application for Federal Student Aid (FAFSA).* Many private colleges and some state schools may also require you to fill out a *Financial Aid Form (FAF).*

All these forms basically ask the same types of questions. They want to know:

The parents' available income
The student's available income
The parents' assets
The student's assets

A "need analysis" is then performed by a company that specializes in this work, to determine what portion of your income and assets you get to keep, and what portion you can afford to give toward college tuition this year. This amount, calculated according to a standard formula, is called the *Expected Family Contribution (EFC).*

The need analysis company sends a report of its findings to your family and, in most cases, to each of the colleges your child has selected. If he's accepted, the school's financial aid officers (FAOs) will decide what they think you can afford, and what you need in the way of grants, work-study, and loans.

Ideally, when your child is accepted at school, you'll also find out how much aid he/she will receive, and what combination of aid the FAO has put together for you.

It's important to know that this figure isn't necessarily carved in stone. You can negotiate with the FAOs. In fact, schools are now expecting parents to negotiate the package, and they don't always make their best offer right away. The more documentation you can provide, the better your chances of convincing them that your need is greater than they've estimated.

Here's a *very* important tip: Although there are tax advantages to making "custodial gift to minors" of up to $10,000 per parent per child per year, *if you think you may be applying for financial aid, never put any money in your child's name.*

Here's why: When you apply for financial aid, and you complete the need analysis form, you have to include both your assets and your child's. The college then assesses these amounts to decide how much you can afford. Your income is assessed up to 47 percent, your assets are assessed up to 5.65 percent. However, your child's income is assessed up to 50 percent and her assets up to 35 percent! So, a college fund of $40,000 in your name is assessed up to $2,260 of that money toward the first year of school. If that same $40,000 was in your child's name, they would figure the child as being able to put $14,000 toward education.

So, if you're pretty sure you won't qualify for financial aid, put the money in your child's name—if it's "iffy," don't. Once it's in your child's name, it's hard to get it out.

If you think you may need help in getting yourself the best deal, you might invest in the services of a *financial aid consultant*, an advisor who will help you fill out the forms, guide you through the application process, and make sure that you look at all options and opportunities. They can also help you to identify other sources of loan programs, private scholarships, and grants. They usually charge fees ranging from $20 to

$500, depending upon what they do. One source of consultants is:

Octameron Associates
P.O. Box 2748
Alexandria, VA 22301
(707) 527-6789

A company that uses a computer database to match your profile to sources of college financing, some of them little known, is:

Guaranteed College Funding
P.O. Box 351
Glenford, NY 12433
(914) 247-0048 (phone and fax)

You can also locate these consultants at a local college or through a high school guidance counselor.

There is another approach toward work and study that's gaining popularity these days, called a *Co-op Program*. This is an interesting way to pay for college and also get a career off to a good start. Students alternate semesters on campus with semesters working at a real job. Each year, now approximately 200,000 students at some 900 colleges do co-op programs. In a typical program, a student takes a responsible job with a company that has agreed to participate in the arrangement. They often work as trainees earning approximately $8,000 to $15,000 a year. Some of this money, minus taxes, will be figured into the financial aid 'needs statement.' Many students find this a boon to their careers, as many of these jobs become full-time after graduation. Technical students have the greatest chance of work, humanities students have a tougher time. Most co-op students are in Business Administration, Computer Science, or other sciences and engineering. While the majority of students work for private business, the federal government has also been a big employer. It put 16,800 students to work in the 1991–1992 school year, and the government usually keeps approximately

45 percent of its students on the payroll after graduation. To learn more, write to:

National Commission for Cooperative Education
360 Huntington Ave.
Boston, MA 02115

Much of the preceding information was adapted from *The Princeton Review Student Access Guide to Paying for College*, 1995 edition, by A. Chany and Geoff Martz, an excellent reference book. The authors state that, as of the present, there exist millions of dollars in unclaimed college funds, if you know where to look. This, of course, is a situation that can't be counted on lasting into the future, but at any time, the more you know and the harder you look, the more chance you have of finding what you're looking for.

Before you figure out your shortfall, include your child's contribution to the college fund:

College Funding with Child's Contribution

	CHILD 1	CHILD 2
College cost		
Child's contribution:		
Savings		
Advanced placement ($ value)		
Scholarship		
Accelerated program ($ value)		
Part-time work		
Other		
Subtotal		
NET TOTAL (TOTAL COST - CHILD'S CONTRIBUTION)		

College Savings Goal with Child's Contribution

Child's Name	Years to College	Estimated Total Cost	College Savings to Date	Needed to Save— Subtotal	Kid's 25%	Needed to Save— Total	Savings per Year

"Savings per year" is simply the amount you need to save, divided by the number of years before your child is ready for college. It doesn't really mean you're going to save the exact same amount each year—it's just a way of keeping track of how far you've gone, how much further you have to go.

Setting Up an Investment Plan for College

Paying for college is easiest if you start early, and as college tuitions go up, this will become ever more true—in fact, it's one of the biggest, one of the very biggest differences between the world today's parents face and the world faced by earlier generations.

If your child is going to be entering college in the next few years and you haven't started saving yet, you're going to have a rough time.

If you're just starting a family now, you really don't have any choice but to think about starting a college investment plan. If you don't, college may actually be out of the question by the time your children are eighteen.

Just look at those numbers I quoted earlier in this chapter on the projected costs of college in the future. If you have a baby born in 1994, and you were to start saving for her college fund now by putting your money in a sock or under the mattress (in other words, no interest), you'd need to put away close to $400 a month to pay her way through Rutgers, nearly $550 a month to pay her way through Howard, and close to $1,200 a month to pay her way through MIT. If you waited until she was ten years old before you started saving, those numbers would be up around $900, $1,200, and $2,700 a month. In other words, you'd need enough socks that someone else would be getting rich buying stock in Hanes, or your mattress would be so lumpy that it would mean a lot of sleepless nights (well, you'd be having those anyway).

What you need to prepare for college is an investment fund.

The best way to build a college investment fund is slowly

and carefully, over time, using conservative investments. If there's a still a shortfall by the time your kids are ready to start applying to college, there are ways you can make it up, but if you try to make too much too fast, and lose your investment, it's your kids who will suffer.

Here's a list of the major investment vehicles, along with my recommendations as to their suitability in a college portfolio:

Table 5: Investment Vehicles

VEHICLE	SUITABILITY FOR COLLEGE PORTFOLIO
Aggressive growth funds	Not OK.
Asset allocation funds	Good because they offer diversification. But their success depends on the ability of the fund managers to time the market.
Balanced funds	Safe investments and good for the beginning investor for college.
Bank money markets	Good in later stages.
CDs	Too conservative in early years, good later on.
Fixed-income mutual funds	OK if you start with the simpler and safer categories—short-term high-grade bond funds and treasuries—then move on to intermediate-term bonds.
Growth funds	Good.
High-grade corporate bonds	OK, but not great. Risk-return factor is not ideally suited for a college plan.

Vehicle	Suitability for college portfolio
Income funds	Good.
Junk bonds	Absolutely not.
Mortgage-backed securities	OK as a part of a diversified portfolio, but don't let them dominate it—and keep in mind that you can't count on a steady stream of payments for the stated life of the investment.
Municipal bonds	Conservative—OK if there's enough time for this slow-but-safe approach.
Stock funds	Good early in investment plan, risky later on.
Taxable money market funds	Good for short term or as you approach paying a large bill.
Tax-exempt money market funds	Good if you're in the higher tax brackets. Otherwise they can be a little too risky, because you're dealing with riskier instruments.
Treasuries	Probably too conservative in terms of yield to be a major part of your college investment program. However, as your child gets closer to college age and you need liquidity and safety, you can consider purchasing some short-term securities.
Unit investment trust	Not great.
Zero-coupon bonds/ baccalaureate bonds	Very good conservative investment for college.*

*You can figure out what you'll be getting from a zero-coupon bond at maturity in *Barron's Parenting Keys: Keys to Investing For Your Child's Future*, by Warren Boroson and Martin S. Shenkman (Barron's Education Series, 1992).

If you know the rate of interest on your investment, you can figure out how much you'll need to invest in order to get back a certain return by a certain time. Here's a table that shows you how to calculate this for investments in bonds.

Table 6: What to Invest to Get Back $1,000

AGE OF CHILD WHEN BOND IS BOUGHT	YIELD				
	6%	7%	8%	9%	10%
birth	$345	$290	$244	$205	$173
5	464	409	361	318	281
13	623	577	534	494	458

Here's how it works. Let's say your child is 5, you want to make sure you have $100,000 for her college fund by the time she's 18, and the current rate of interest on a thirteen-year zero-coupon is 8 percent. If you invest $361 now, you'll have $1,000 in thirteen years. So to get the $100,000, you'd have to invest $36,100.

In building something as important as a portfolio for college, of course, your best bet is to sit down with a qualified financial planner and come up with a realistic plan, given your budget and financial expectations.

Still, there are some general guidelines you can follow.

In the ideal world, if you have started saving from birth, you'll have eighteen years for a savings program. In that case, an overall strategy to consider is to put the money in long-term growth mutual funds and start to think about turning it into more and more liquidity as time draws closer to college. When your child is approximately five years from the start of college, move to low-rise income creating investments, such as bank CDs and money market mutual funds or short-term bonds.

If you do start early, invest in growth stocks. Only stocks can be counted on to grow fast enough over the long term to meet your goals. Over the past sixty-eight years, the shares of large blue chip companies returned an average of 10.3 percent a year (pretax). During the same period, stocks of smaller companies had a return of 12.4 percent. So, with blue chips, your money doubles in seven years, and with small stocks, it doubles in six years. Also, over the same sixty-eight years, risk-free investments such as treasury bills gained only 3.7 percent.

Still, although stocks work for the long term, they're too volatile to be good in the short term, so as college approaches, move out of growth stocks into bonds and more stable investments.

WITH A LONG TIME (15–20 YEARS) TO COLLEGE

Invest in growth stock mutual funds.

Try to set up automatic investment each month.

Spread money among several funds.

Avoid gimmicks that call themselves "ideal college investments."

Think about money in your child's name. There are a couple of ways to do this, such as a type of custodial account called the *Universal Gift to Minors Act (UGMA)* or *Uniform Transfer to Minors Act (UTMA)*. The tax code says that if your child is under 14, the first $600 is taxed at his/her rate, usually 15 percent, and any dividends and interest received by the child is then taxed at your rate. Once the child turns 14, however, the income is taxed at his or her rate. The good news here is that there may be a tax savings. The bad news—at age 18, this money legally becomes the child's. If a Ferrari looks better than four years of college, you may have a problem.

If you feel uneasy about the custodial account, you can consider sitting up a minor's trust. The first $3,600 of its income is taxed at the 15 percent rate and additional earn-

ings at 28 percent up to $10,900 and 31 percent thereafter.
With 15–20 years to go, this is a good mix:

    60% capital stock funds
    15% international stocks
    10% long-term bonds
    10% intermediate-term bonds
     5% cash equivalent

WITH 10 YEARS OR MORE TO COLLEGE

You're still in a basically long-term pattern. The variation
here has to do with your own risk tolerance, but essentially
you're looking at two types of funds: a combination of two-
thirds growth (strong earnings potential), one-third value
(stocks that are trading on the market under their real value).
Your holdings should look something like this:

    65% U.S. growth stock funds
    15% international funds (half in emerging markets)
    10% bond fund/fixed income
    10% CDs

    or this:

    40% capital stock funds
    10% international stocks
    10% long-term bonds
    25% intermediate-term bonds
    15% short-term bonds

WITH 5 YEARS TO COLLEGE

It's time to start being more cautious. You can't suffer big
losses now, because there's no time to recover from them. If
you're starting out now, you'll have to start with caution. If

you're heavily into stocks and the market falls, there'll be no time to recover.

As your child hits his teens, you should be starting to move 15 percent of your stock into more conservative investments, in a pattern like this:

40% in low-risk equities
Remainder in U.S. Treasuries

The majority of your fixed income belongs in securities with an average maturity of ten years or less. Ibbotson says that a small portion can be allocated to higher yielding long-term issues by heavily weighting bond holdings to intermediate- and short-term issues. In this way you'll avoid steep losses if rates climb sharply.

If you're in the 28 percent tax bracket, tax-exempt municipal bonds can be more advantageous than treasuries.

Some parents may want to use Series EE U.S. Savings Bonds for college (see Chapter 9).

WITH 2 YEARS TO COLLEGE

Start cashing in stock funds. By this point, you should have no more than 10 percent in stocks; by your child's sophomore year in college you should be out of them completely.

Keep 5 percent in short-term bond funds with maturities of 4 years of less.

Just before college payments start, switch your cash to a money market fund so you can write checks against it. Put the rest of your assets in CDs that mature in time for your child's junior and senior year.

A good portfolio should look like this:

35% capital stock funds
10% long-term bonds
30% intermediate-term bonds
25% short term-bonds or CDs

Here's a worksheet to chart your investments, projected and actual.

Investments for College

INVESTMENT	BEGINNING OF YEAR	END OF YEAR	NET GAIN OR LOSS
Investment A			
Investment B			
Investment C			
Investment D			
Investment E			
TOTAL			

You'll do an "Investments for College" worksheet like this for each year that you're saving for college. The totals for each of those worksheets will provide the figures for the middle three columns in the next worksheet. "Needed to save" comes from the College Savings Goal with Child's Contribution worksheet. The final column, "Still needed," is "End-of-year portfolio" subtracted from "Needed to save."

Your College Investment Portfolio

Year	Needed to Save	Beginning of Year Portfolio	Profit or Loss for Year	End of Year Portfolio	Still Needed
1996					
1997					
1998					
1999					
2000					
2001					
2002					
2003					
2004					
2005					
2006					
2007					
2008					
2009					
2010					

(continued on next page)

YEAR	NEEDED TO SAVE	BEGINNING OF YEAR PORTFOLIO	PROFIT OR LOSS FOR YEAR	END OF YEAR PORTFOLIO	STILL NEEDED
2011					
2012					
2013					
2014					

Keep one of these worksheets for each child. Make up this worksheet when you start saving for your child's college fund, so you'll know where you have to go. Keep maintaining and updating it regularly.

If, as time goes on, you develop a more accurate projection of what college will cost, that goes into the College Funding and College Savings Goal worksheets and the College Investment Portfolio worksheet. Or, your college cost estimate may change completely. If your financial picture gets better, you may want to upgrade the choice of colleges your child can try for; if you have unexpected hardships, you may have to step back.

In any case, the bottom line—the lower right-hand corner of your worksheet—is the figure you have to keep watching. If that figure is going to be lower than the figure in the College Savings Goal worksheet, then you'll have to think about alternative ways of making up the difference.

A Few More Money-Saving Tips

Not choosing the right college can cost you money: Transferring can mean a significant expense, including lost credits, yet approximately 60 percent of the students who enter college as freshman do not graduate from that school. Most leave because they realize they chose the wrong college.

There's no guarantee that a college will live up to a student's expectations, but there are ways of improving the odds.

Visit each school first. Comparison shopping makes as much sense for a $200,000 investment in college as it does for a $500 investment in a stereo . . . even more. Go with your child, and have him go alone to meet with students and faculty. Do the students share his interests? Nothing changes faster than the interests of a college freshman; still, he can get some idea of whether he's likely to find kindred souls.

Even if interests change, levels of ability and intellectual curiosity may be predicted. Compare your child's high school grade point average with the average for this year's freshmen. College admissions officers will give you the data. If his scores are higher than the average, he may find himself underchallenged.

Look at the school's program in your child's planned major. If science is his focus, for example, find out if the labs have up-to-date equipment, if the libraries have a wide range of scientific periodicals and a better than adequate holding of new books in the field. Find out what science majors do after graduation. It's a good sign if many get into prestigious graduate schools or win scholarships.

Take note of class sizes. At small colleges, the ratio of students to faculty members is a sound indicator of how much personal attention your child will get in general, but what about courses in his major? Ask an admissions officer to estimate those class sizes. A ratio of ten students per teacher is excellent.

Going to school near home may save you money. Twenty-two states give promising native sons and daughters financial incentives to go to local state schools. Usually, this means a grade point average of at least 3.0 in high school and a family income of no more than a certain amount (varies by state). Some states will also partially pay for private schools in their state. Call your state's Department of Higher Education for more information on these programs.

And, needless to say, a college near home offers the opportunity to live at home and commute, which can save on travel as well as room and board expenses . . . and it can mean a few more years of having someone there to take out the garbage!

You may save money by keeping it all in the family. Certain colleges and universities offer a discount to tuition for the second member of the family that enrolls. Others will give a special deal to children of alumni.

You might want to prepay. Many colleges are offering a prepayment plan, a large discount on your child's tuition if you sign her up years in advance of her coming of college age and contribute funds to that college.

This has some obvious problems. What if your child doesn't want to go to that college? What if she can't get into it?

You may want to look into the program anyway. But if you do, consider a couple of other questions: Is it the best allocation of funds? Does the discount you'll get from the college create a better bottom line than you'll get from investing the money elsewhere?

And what happens to that money if your child doesn't go to the college into which you've been prepaying?

Making Up the Rest

How do you come up with the extra money?

I've put this last on the agenda, and there's a reason.

This should be the last thing you think about.

Applying for financial aid, or any form of borrowing, should only be a way of making up a shortfall between what you have and what you need, never a first alternative. It can be a big debt, and it may come at a tough time. College may hit on your time line when you should be gearing up for retirement, and that's not the ideal time to incur debt.

Still, there may well be a shortfall, especially if you have gotten a late start in saving for college.

Pragmatically, the first thing you should do when confronted with a shortfall is reassess your goals. Are they realistic? Maybe your child will have to go to a state school, rather than a private college. Maybe he should consider starting out at a community college, then transferring. This can be a considerably cheaper alternative. But make sure, if your child is starting out at a two-year college, that he's taking courses that will be transferable toward a four-year degree. (If you realize these truths early on, be realistic with your kids. Don't raise their expectations unrealistically, encouraging them to apply to a private college, or a four-year college, when you know that they won't be able to go even if they are accepted.)

One way to judge a two-year college is to see if they have a chapter of Phi Theta Kappa, the honor society considered the two-year counterpart of Phi Beta Kappa.

A couple of good sources on community colleges are: *The Best 286 Colleges* (Villard, $17), which explains how you can get the most out of a community college. *Transferring Made Easy* (Peterson's, $11.95) gives nuts-and-bolts information on transferring to a four-year college. Peterson's *Guide to Two-Year Colleges* is a solid all-around source.

Here are some of the ways you can go about making up the shortfall:

A college loan that's available to parents is the federal Parents Loans to Undergraduate Students (PLUS). The 1994/95 rate was 8.38 percent and you can apply for it through a bank or other private lender. A PLUS loan can cover the full cost of your child's education minus financial aid, and the interest rate is often 1 to 3 percentage points lower than what private lenders charge. Moreover, up-front fees on PLUS (as well as on Stafford Loans) now total only 4 percent, down from 8 percent in 1993/94.

To qualify for PLUS you must have no loan delinquencies of more than ninety days, and your child must be attending college at least half-time (more than twelve classroom hours per week). While private lenders will still make most federal loans in 1995, in 1996 about 500 colleges will be enrolled in the new Federal Direct Student Loan Program. Students at those schools and their parents will be eligible for Stafford or PLUS dispenses by the U.S. Department of Education. By 1998, the department hopes to make this program available at 60 percent of colleges. One potential drawback to this system is that although loans will be approved faster, borrowers will have to pay a 1 percent insurance fee and they won't be able to get a rate discount from Sallie Mae.

If you have to take out a loan, here are the possible ways you can do it, listed in order of the best to the worst. But remember, any loan has to be paid back, has to be paid back with interest, and has to be collateralized, which means you're putting something at risk.

Here's a tip: If you plan to supplement financial aid with a home equity loan or second mortgage, get the loan first. Many schools take the value of your home equity into account when calculating your family's financial need. The outstanding home equity loan reduces your equity and may boost your chances to qualify for need-based grants and scholarships.

If There's No Way

Sometimes there's just nothing you can do. You started saving too late. You had a horrendous financial setback. Your child just doesn't want to go to college, and the truth is, he just isn't college material.

We know the widening income gap between college and non-college graduates, but there are many job openings requiring skills that you can acquire on the job or from technical schools. Aircraft technicians can get a job from a 2½-year program earning $30,000+. Computer programmers can earn $25,000 after a six-month course. Technical training is expensive, but cheaper than four years of college. Many two-year

TYPE OF LOAN	HOW IT WORKS	WHY YOU'D WANT TO	WHAT TO BE CAREFUL OF	RECOMMENDATION
Home equity loan	As a line of credit worth up to 80% of your home equity, you can draw money from the fund whenever tuition is due. Usually has a variable interest rate. As a lump sum, with monthly repayments; usually a fixed interest rate.	Generally relatively low interest. Interest is deductible.	Shop around for best interest rates, application fees, closing costs. Remember that you're putting your house at risk.	Generally a good choice.
Refinancing home mortgage	A new mortgage pays off the existing mortgage, so if your mortgage has been paid off, you'll pocket the difference (less various costs).	Probably only if you were planning to do it anyway, to take advantage of favorable mortgage rates.	Refinancing costs are typically 3 to 5%. It can be a slow process, as slow as getting a first mortgage.	Only if you have other reasons to want to refinance —otherwise a home equity loan is the better choice.
Borrowing against stocks and bonds	You'd take out a "margin loan" from brokerage firm, typically up to 50% of the value of your securities—if you hold U.S Treasuries, up to 90%.	Not as cheap a loan as a home equity, but the next best—and you're not putting up your house. You can deduct some interest, but not as much as a home equity.	Possibility of a "margin call" if your securities drop in value —this means you have to come up with cash to make up the difference, or lose your collateral.	This might be a second alternative if you decide against a home equity loan.

(continued on next page)

Type of loan	How it works	Why you'd want to	What to be careful of	Recommendation
Personal loan	From a bank. This can be an unsecured loan, based on your earning capacity or net worth, or a secured loan, in which you put up specific assets as capital.	If your alternative is to cash in securities, this saves you early withdrawal penalties.	Not the best interest rate, no tax advantage.	Probably not a good choice.
Loans against life insurance	You can borrow up to the full amount of the cash value of your whole life insurance policy from your insurer.	If you keep up interest payments, no pressure to pay back the principal.	If you die with an outstanding loan, your beneficiaries will get the face value of the policy minus the unpaid loan.	A special kind of risk here—you may be risking your family's future security.
Loans from retirement plans	If you participate in 401(k) or other retirement plans, you can typically take out as much as half of your vested balance or $50,00, whichever is less (see your company's benefits department for details).	Truthfully, only as a last resort.	You must pay it back within five years, with interest. Otherwise, the loan is considered a withdrawal and you'll owe regular income taxes plus a 10% penalty. If you leave your job, you'll have to pay it back in full.	Not a good choice. Interest rates don't compare with a home equity loan, there are no tax breaks, and if you're not careful there can be serious tax penalties.

(continued on next page)

Type of loan	How it works	Why you'd want to	What to be careful of	Recommendation
Credit card loans	You stick your card in the ATM machine, or write a check, and they give you the money.	Well, it's fast. Outside of that, has absolutely nothing to recommend it.	At the very best, humongous interest rates.	Do not choose this option under any circumstances.

community colleges and private junior colleges offer technical training. Tuition averages approximately $1,000–$2,000 a year for such job-oriented studies as data processing, real estate sales, police sciences, auto mechanics, etc.

Hands-on training is very important. Many high-tech companies will educate and pay an employee at the same time. Some will even pay high school students. The Labor Department's Bureau of Apprenticeship and Training supervises approximately 45,000 apprenticeship programs. They include plumbers, pipefitters, carpenters, biomedical equipment technicians, meteorologists, chefs, etc.

You can earn a four-year degree (B.A.) entirely by mail or phone . . . and computer technology is making non-resident learning even more of reality. Most correspondence programs require some classroom attendance. I know of one that doesn't. It is the Center for Distance Learning at Empire State College, part of the State University of New York. Credits cost approximately $100 and as a matriculated student you need 128 to graduate. For information, write to:

> The Center for Distance Learning
> Empire State College
> 2 Union Ave.
> Saratoga Springs, NY 12866

Sometimes you can even earn college credits for life experience: learning you have acquired on your own. I did . . . sometimes it seems as though I did everything in the world to get through college, but this was extreme even for me. At 18, through an odd combination of circumstances, I found myself the only American woman civilian in Vietnam. When I came back to college, I was able to turn the trip into credit for my degree.

To earn credit, you can take standardized tests, or sometimes the college will tailor an exam. For more information, contact:

College Level Examination Program (CLEP)
College Board
45 Columbus Ave.
New York, NY 10023
(212) 713-8064

Time Line 5

	1996	1997	1998	1999	2000	2001	2002	2003
Total current expenses								
Total baby expenses								
Total child care expenses								
Total shelter expenses (ongoing)								
TOTAL EXPENSES								
TOTAL INCOME								
TOTAL SAVINGS								
Cash outlay from savings: shelter								
Cash outlay from savings: college								
NET SAVINGS								
TARGET SAVINGS								
CLOSENESS TO TARGET GOAL +/–								

2004	2005	2006	2007	2008	2009	2010	2011	2012	2013

The new rows here bring your college spending and savings figures into the picture. We've added a row called "Cash outlay from savings: college," which gives you a place to enter your next major withdrawal on your savings. And after "Net savings," I've put in two more rows: "Target savings," the amount of money you'll need to have saved at any given point along your time line to be on schedule for meeting your major expenses; and "Closeness to savings goal," which is a reference point to tell you how you're doing.

Sue and Dan

Sue and Dan are figuring their college savings needs on the basis of one child going to an expensive private college and one child going to a state college. This is a sort of a middle-ground strategy. They can upgrade to two private college tuitions if they start doing better financially, or cut back if they suffer financial reversals.

Sue and Dan: Savings Goal

CHILD'S NAME	YEARS TO COLLEGE	ESTIMATED TOTAL COST	COLLEGE SAVINGS TO DATE	NEEDED TO SAVE	SAVINGS PER YEAR
Child 1	20	$260,000	0	$260,000	$13,000
Child 2	22	95,000	0	95,000	4,300

Sue and Dan: College Funding with Child's Contribution

	CHILD 1	CHILD 2
College cost	$260,000	$95,000
Child's contribution:		
Savings		
Advanced placement ($ value)		
Scholarship		
Accelerated program ($ value)		
Part-time work		
Other		
Subtotal	65,000	24,000
NET TOTAL (TOTAL COST - CHILD'S CONTRIBUTION)	**195,000**	**72,000**

At this point, Sue and Dan can only fill in the bottom lines of this worksheet. The details will have to wait until their children get older.

Sue and Dan: College Savings Goal with Child's Contribution

Child's Name	Years to College	Estimated Total Cost	College Savings to Date	Needed to Save— Subtotal	Kid's 25%	Needed to Save— Total	Savings per Year
Child 1	20	$260,000	0	$260,000	$65,000	$195,000	$10,000
Child 2	22	95,000	0	95,000	24,000	71,000	3,200

Sue and Dan have once again stretched their time line further out in the future—far enough to cover their next foreseeable major expense, which will be their children's college fund. They've also added another row, "Cash outlay from savings: college" and entered the figures that they'll have to draw down each year when their children are in college.

"Target savings," at this point, represents the "Needed to save" figure from the College Savings Goal worksheet, for both children together. If Sue and Dan were planning to buy a house further down the line, they might incorporate that in their "Needed to save" figure, too, but because it comes so near the beginning of their time line, they decided it wasn't necessary.

Their "Savings per year column" only just reflects savings, not investment. The reason is that it's simply too speculative to make up a theoretical investment table for Sue and Dan. It's for this reason, in fact, that we're bidding a fond farewell to Sue and Dan with this chapter. The rest of the subject matter, such as a long-term inverstment strategy, doesn't lend itself to a hypothetical couple. So we'll wish Sue and Dan good luck, thank them for their help, and trust that they'll go on filling in their worksheets on their own.

Sue and Dan Time Line 5

	1996	1997	1998	1999	2000	2001	2002	2003
Total current expenses	25,000	25,000	30,000	45,000	50,000	50,000	50,000	50,000
Total baby expenses		11,800		10,100				
Total child care expenses	5,300	5,300	10,100	6,500	6,500	1,700	1,700	1,700
Total shelter expenses (ongoing)	30,000	30,000	30,000	23,000	23,000	23,000	23,000	23,000
TOTAL EXPENSES	55,000	66,800	65,300	83,400	83,100	79,500	79,500	74,700
TOTAL NET INCOME	**73,200**	**76,860**	**76,860**	**84,180**	**84,180**	**84,180**	**84,180**	**84,180**
SAVINGS PER YEAR	**18,200**	**10,100**	**12,100**	**1,300**	**1,600**	**5,200**		
SAVINGS TO DATE	**15,000**	**33,200**	**43,300**	**34,400**	**35,700**	**37,300**		
Cash outlay from savings: shelter			**21,000**					
Cash outlay from savings: college								
NET SAVINGS	**33,200**	**43,300**	**34,400**	**35,700**	**37,300**	**42,500**		
TARGET SAVINGS	**13,300**	**26,600**	**39,900**	**53,200**	**66,500**	**79,800**	**93,100**	**106,400**
CLOSENESS TO SAVINGS GOAL +/-	**19,900**	**16,700**	**<5,500>**	**<17,500>**	**<29,200>**			

2004	2005	2006	2007	2008		2015	2016	2017	2018
50,000	50,000	50,000	50,000	50,000		50,000	50,000	50,000	50,000
23,000	23,000	23,000	23,000	23,000		23,000	23,000	23,000	23,000
74,700	74,700								
84,180	**84,180**								
						49,000	49,000	67,000	67,000
119,700	**133,000**	**146,300**	**159,600**	**172,900**		**266,000**			

7

Enrichment

Enrichment, by my definition, is everything that will contribute to making your children more civilized—to making them broader, more complete people, better citizens, and more fulfilled as individuals. Enrichment, in general, falls into four categories:

Educational
Cultural
Physical
Spiritual

You should be aware that it is up to you to give your children the opportunity to broaden themselves in all these areas. You have the mandate, and, since all of these areas of enrichment are subjective and personal, you have the power to define them, structure them to fit them into your own vision and lifestyle.

Don't forget: If you don't plan enrichments, they won't happen. Or: If you don't plan them, *something* will happen, but it won't be what you expected, and it may get totally out of hand. I call this the "water torture approach" to destroying a

family budget: something that starts out innocently and inex-
pensively, like a dripping faucet. But it keeps going, one
droplet at a time, nothing that's impossible to tolerate by
itself, but before you know it, it's turned into a trickle, and
finally a gush of money and time that's drawing all your
resources. Eight-year-old Johnny wants to play soccer? What
could possibly be the harm? Ten bucks for a soccer ball from
Wal-Mart, an afternoon a week picking him up from an after-
school soccer program. Suddenly, it's five years later, and he
needs a uniform, state-of-the-art soccer shoes, a regulation
ball (you mean the ten-dollar Wal-Mart model isn't regulation?), special soccer lessons, soccer camp, plus he's going to
the state championships which are in Sacramento and you
live in San Diego, and the whole family is expected to come
up and watch him play.

And soccer is a relatively inexpensive sport!

Not to say that it can't all be wonderful. But it may be a *lot*
more of a commitment than you expected.

Enrichment is an area where a lot of the financial planning
concepts we talked about earlier come into play, and in ways
that you might not expect. Fixed *vs.* variable expense, opportunity costs, return on investment in connection with Hebrew
school, cello lessons, or karate training?

Absolutely. If you don't plan, you have no control over the
outcome. And these are the tools of planning.

Your Dream List

Let's start where we started before . . . with a dream list. You
can have anything in dreams, so put down everything you'd
like your kids to have, in each category of enrichment.

Education, generally speaking, is the kind of thing that
schools offer, but perhaps they don't offer enough, because of
budget cutbacks or because your child has a special interest
that goes beyond what the school has to offer. This might

include foreign language studies, or science, or our country's heritage, or the heritage of your own and other ethnic groups, or nature and environmental studies . . . whatever is important to you and your family.

For purposes of making up your financial worksheets, I'm including private schooling in this chapter. Of course, education is a need, not a want. But private school education is a variable expense—you have to decide whether it will be part of your budget. The costs of private schools, and what they offer—what you'd want them for—vary so widely that your best bet here is individual research.

For some families—this was certainly true for me—education and shelter expenses must be balanced against each other. If you live in a place where public schools aren't adequate, private schools can be one option; moving can be another.

Culture can include music, art, the theater, studying the cultural heritage of various peoples, crafts, exploring your own creative potential.

Physical fitness includes all sorts of sports and exercise programs, hiking, camping, outdoor activities.

Spiritual enrichment can include religious studies, participation in religious organization–sponsored youth groups, reading to a blind person, working as a volunteer in a homeless shelter, or whatever your family turns to for enhancement of its spirituality.

One place where there's a possibility of your children receiving some or all of the above is in summer camp. I'll discuss that later in this chapter.

It's important to note here that your children will eventually begin to structure their own enrichment programs; they'll be drawn to their own interests. You can help provide a basis for this by giving them the broadest possible exposure when they're young.

Tad, my co-author, recalls three trips he made to Washington, D.C., with his daughters, when they were 13, 10, and 9—separate trips to visit an elderly aunt who wanted to see the children, but felt that seeing them all at the same time would be too much for her.

"I went down three times within a month and a half," he recalls, "and I went to three different cities."

Each girl set her own itinerary. Charis, who went on to become a lawyer, wanted to visit the Supreme Court and the Capitol building. Caitlin chose the Smithsonian and the National Gallery; she went on to major in drama in college and has published short stories. Wendy, who is now a college administrator, wanted to see historical landmarks like the Jefferson Memorial (where in later years, her husband-to-be proposed to her) and Ford's Theater.

Expenses or commitments for enrichment will fall into the following general categories: instruction, hardware, software, travel, and time.

Instruction is tutoring, coaching, workshops, seminars—whatever involves going to some other person for the imparting of specialized information. This can be as varied as Spanish lessons, basketball camp, guitar or chess or computer graphics lessons, Hebrew school, SAT prep classes, or any one of a thousand things that people are available to teach.

Hardware is equipment: microscopes, stereos, saddles and bridles, clarinets, computers, oscilloscopes.

Software is equipment, too, sort of. It's the kind that you need to keep replenishing, that you use with the hardware: sheet music, computer programs, oil paints, specimen bottles and microscope slides, duct tape.

Travel is anything you go to that costs something, whether it's driving the family into the city to see an exhibit of Egyptian art or driving Junior to baseball practice; sending the kids off to camp or sending your young cello prodigy to San Juan for the Pablo Casals festival.

Time is time; it's a finite resource, and the trip to Calaveras County so that your daughter can enter her pet in the annual frog-jumping contest is time that you're not spending doing anything else. If you have more than one child, it's important to make sure that you allocate equal time to all their enrichment projects. Remember that money isn't the only commodity for which you have to figure opportunity costs. Your time is an opportunity cost, too, and you must choose where and how to use it.

When you start making up your enrichment worksheets, if you're at all confused about what category to put something in, *don't worry about it.* Is that course in the history of the blues educational or cultural? If a tennis racket is hardware, are tennis balls hardware or software? Is a yoga class physical fitness or spiritual enrichment? Who cares? It's your list. These categories are just guidelines so you don't forget anything; they're not a test.

Once you've made your dream list—where you literally put down everything you can think of that you'd like to expose your children to—then you can start to put all of it into a budget—a money budget and a time budget. For your dream list, think about what it will take to give your kids a healthy exposure to a particular enrichment activity. If your child wants to take something to the next level, then you'll have to figure out what the long-term budgetary implications are.

Be as detailed or as broad as you want here. If you think it would be a good idea for the family to take in a concert once a month, put that down; if you want your family to be exposed to a wide range of music, so that you'll want to rotate the concerts between classical, jazz, blues, and folk, put that down.

Educational Enrichment

ITEM	FAMILY OR INDIVIDUAL	HOW OFTEN?	TIME PER EVENT	TIME PER MONTH	COST PER EVENT	COST PER MONTH	COST PER YEAR

(continued on next page)

ITEM	FAMILY OR INDIVIDUAL	HOW OFTEN?	TIME PER EVENT	TIME PER MONTH	COST PER EVENT	COST PER MONTH	COST PER YEAR

Cultural Enrichment

ITEM	FAMILY OR INDIVIDUAL	HOW OFTEN?	TIME PER EVENT	TIME PER MONTH	COST PER EVENT	COST PER MONTH	COST PER YEAR

Physical Enrichment

ITEM	FAMILY OR INDIVIDUAL	HOW OFTEN?	TIME PER EVENT	TIME PER MONTH	COST PER EVENT	COST PER MONTH	COST PER YEAR

Spiritual Enrichment

ITEM	FAMILY OR INDIVIDUAL	HOW OFTEN?	TIME PER EVENT	TIME PER MONTH	COST PER EVENT	COST PER MONTH	COST PER YEAR

Total Enrichment

ITEM	TIME PER EVENT	TIME PER MONTH	COST PER EVENT	COST PER MONTH	COST PER YEAR	YEARS OF EXPENSE	YEARS TO EXPENSE
Total family enrichment							
Total individual enrichment (each family member)							
Total individual enrichment (total—adding everyone together)							
TOTAL ENRICHMENT							

Now, how many of these can you actually budget into your lives? Time and money are both finite resources. If there's not enough time or money to do everything, don't worry about it. You should have dreams on a grand scale—as Robert Browning wrote, "A man's reach should exceed his grasp—or what's a heaven for?"

Here's where we look at some of our cost-accounting techniques, and we find that if you try to apply bean-counting principles to these most un-bean-countable subjects of social and intellectual and spiritual development—surprise! It really works!

Let's take a look:

Opportunity cost: If there's only so much money/time, then an asset that's allocated in one place isn't going to be there to allocate somewhere else. You must think about this when you're thinking about committing to something—or when you're about to commit youself to something without thinking about it.

And, while we're on the subject, don't forget—time spent watching television has an opportunity cost. That's potential enrichment time, and if you're allocating it to "Beavis and Butthead," you're taking it away from something else.

Return on investment: This is the really important one. You've already charted costs. Now, can you chart what you'll be getting in return for that outlay of time and money?

To some extent, you can. Keep in mind that numbers aren't the whole story here—finally, you're going to have to look to your heart, and to your intuitive sense of what's important for you and your kids. But you can create at least a rough gauge for that intuition, like this:

For each item on your enrichment dream lists, fill out one of these Enrichment Return on Investment worksheets. For the *Value* column, put down how much you think this particular enrichment program will help in each of the following categories, using the following scale:

0 = not relevant
1 = slight impact
2 = moderate impact
3 = significant impact

For *Priority*, you have two choices—*1* for normal priority, *2* for high priority. For your *Subtotal* figure, multiply Value times Priority. Your *Total* figure is the sum of all the Subtotals.

And keep one more very important thing in mind: If, when you've finished this exercise, the numbers feel wrong, there's a good chance they are wrong. Look at them again. But maybe your numbers are right—you've learned something about your enrichment priorities that you didn't know.

If the numbers are wrong, then do them again, until they feel right. Maybe some of my categories really aren't significant to you, and you'll want to cut them out. Maybe some of them are so important that you really want to divide them into separate and equal subcategories. Remember . . . they're only numbers, and they're *your* numbers.

Enrichment Return On Investment

ENRICHMENT PROGRAM:			
WAYS THIS PROGRAM CAN HELP	VALUE	PRIORITY	SUBTOTAL
Help in getting college scholarship			
Leadership and social interaction benefits			
Increased sensitivity to environment and humanity			
Improve thinking/problem solving skills			

(continued on next page)

Enrichment program:			
Ways this program can help	Value	Priority	Subtotal
Physical health and endurance			
Cultural literacy			
Self-esteem			
Total			

Now you have to get down to serious number-crunching. Well, maybe the number-crunching isn't so serious—you can do it without a computer. But the prioritizing is plenty significant. You have your return on investment charts for each of your enrichment programs. Which activities rate so high that you *have* to find room in your budget for them? Those are the ones that are the equivalent of fixed-expense items: You'll find room in your budget for them. On the next tier are the activities that you'd like to find a place for. These are the variable-expense items; you'll make room for them when you can.

Long-range Planning

Some items on your enrichment program—reading a good book a week, a family trip to a place of historical interest, volunteering a block of time at a local homeless shelter—may remain a more or less constant part of your enrichment schedule and your enrichment budget.

Other items are going to change, and one of the main reasons for change will be that your children will grow up, and they'll go through phases where they have sudden, short-lived passionate interests, and they'll also start developing their mature personalities, which means they'll have serious, long-term interests.

You'll now have to begin charting your family's enrichment budget a little differently. You can still budget time and money for doing things as a family, although as your children get to be teenagers, there'll be fewer and fewer of those.

For your children's individual enrichment activities, you're going to have to make a different kind of budget, a fairly simple one. You'll have to make a total budget line for each of your kids—how much money can you spend supporting their enrichment? And how much time can you give per child?

Then, it will be your kids' turn to sit down and make out their own worksheets, just like the ones above. And it will be your task to tell them what you can contribute and explain to them that after that, they're on their own. They have to make up the financial difference themselves, and they can't count on you for rides, or to show up for any more than a certain number of games and recitals. Maybe you can make everything if you have an only child—but if you have more than one, make sure that you're giving to all what you give to each.

Resources

Learning Vacations, by Gerson C. Eisenberg (Peterson's Guides, Princeton, N.J., $11.98), is a wonderful tribute to the concept that vacations can exercise the mind as well as the body. The chapters, arranged state by state and listing vactions in foreign countries as well, cover a wide range of subjects, many of which are suitable for whole families.

Programs, accommodations, and costs are covered. Following are some representative entries from the different chapters:

Seminars and Workshops On and Off Campus: "Study programs for individuals and families on campuses and elsewhere in the United States and Canada. The experience of sharing one's knowledge, in and out of the classroom, with others of diverse backgrounds is always rewarding."
A sample entry:

The Chautauqua Institution
Schools Office
P.O. Box 1098
Chautauqua, NY 14722

Special studies courses [one day to nine weeks] include handicrafts, foreign languages, language arts and literature, basic skills of learning, cultural and behavioral studies, practical daily skills, recreation, exercise, and more. Programs for children ages two and up.

Journeys Far and Near: "Sightseeing with a purpose. This chapter includes cultural journeys and trips led by cultural specialists to all areas of the globe."
A sample entry:

Washington Insider Student Tours, Inc.
2424 Pennsylvania Ave. NW, Suite 814
Washington, D.C. 20037

Educational student and adult group tours of Washington, D.C., and environs ... sightseeing for first time visitors, selected itinerary for social studies classes ... usually includes a visit to a congressional representative ... children aged 6 and over may participate. ... Costs, including area transportation, hotel stay, and two meals, range from approximately $50 to $75 per day.

Archaeology, Science, and History: "Viewing historic sites or exploring the past by digging its relics provides fun, excitement and adventure while offering the reward of an enhanced knowledge of history and science."

A sample entry:

Arizona Archaeological Society
P.O. Box 9665
Phoenix, AZ 86058

Field school at Elden Pueblo, a Sinagua ruin dating from A.D. 1100 to 1275. Participants are involved in work at all levels of excavation . . . as well as in a laboratory class; 1–2 weeks, June–August. . . . Children may accompany their parents; they must have the director's approval to participate. . . . Cost: Tuition $5 per week. AAS membership $12 per year (family membership, $17 per year).

The Great Outdoors: "Learning vacations for the adventurous of all ages who enjoy the natural environment. . . . Learn outdoor skills and survival techniques while discovering more about ecological systems and the wildlife they support."

A sample entry:

Canyonlands Field Institute
P.O. Box 68
Moab, Utah 84532

Canyonlands EDventures, 1–7 days, spring-fall. Seminars and outings in natural history, geology, prehistoric cultures, literature, landscape photography, and outdoor education. . . . Children welcome on most programs. . . . Cost $35 per person on day trips, $50–100 per person per day on longer trips; includes meals, rooms, and outfitter fees when appropriate.

Arts, Crafts, and Photography: "Shaping and capturing the world with your hands and eyes. . . . These programs offer both beginner and professional an opportunity to improve their skills and to unleash their creativity."

A sample entry:

WoodenBoat Publications
WoodenBoat School
P.O. Box 78
Brooklin, Maine 04616

Courses in boatbuilding, woodworking, marine-related crafts, and seamanship; 1 and 2 weeks, June–October. . . . Children over 12 . . . in some courses; otherwise, the minimum age is 16. Cost: Tuition, $350–400; room and board, $195 per week. A scholarship amounting to one-third of the tuition cost is offered in every course.

Music, Dance, and Drama: "Experience the arts through a fascinating variety of worldwide educational and entertainment opportunities—as participant or spectator."

A sample entry:

New Orleans Jazz and Heritage Festival
P.O. Box 53407
New Orleans, LA 70153–3407

Last weekend in April through first weekend in May . . . a wide variety of music, including jazz, rock, blues, gospel and more. There are crafts exhibits, the Afro-American market, parades, and evening jazz concerts . . . the festival is a national event and one of the outstanding cultural celebrations in the world.

Museums and Historical Society Exhibits and Trips: "As repositories of artistic treasures and records of the past, museums and historical societies function for the benefit of current and future generations. Participants experience the world's great artistic and cultural treasures through their exhibits and local programs."

A sample entry:

Museum of Arts and Sciences
1040 Museum Boulevard
Daytona Beach, FL 32014

Summer Science Institute for children ages 9–12, with field trip–oriented classes focusing on a diverse range of natural science subjects, including marine science, paleontology, archaeology, astronomy, insect and shell studies . . . $65 per one-week session.

Of course, fees and tuitions may increase; these selections are just to give an idea of the range of enrichment programs available.

The range of enrichment-oriented vacations is virtually endless.

The Dinosaur Society's Guide to Vacationing with Dinosaurs, available from the society, (800) 346-6366, $5, gives a complete rundown on dinosaur digs in the United States and Canada, including camping information and where you can hike in fossil footprints.

Want to share with your sports-loving kids a fast-shrinking piece of Americana, where baseball is still played close to the fans, by non-millionaires? *Minor Trips* (P.O. Box 360105, Strongsville, OH 44136) gives a state-by-state guide to minor league baseball games.

Enrichment: A Personal Note

The wonderful thing about enrichment is that it really lives up to its name: It's wonderful, and it enriches your life. Here's an example from my own experience:

When my kids were little, I bought them art books for children, the kind the Metropolitan Museum of Art sells in its gift shop, with stickers of great paintings to put on the appropriate page, and a little article about the artist and the painting below where the sticker went. I gave them the books; they seemed to like them. I didn't know if it meant anything more than that, but I had a little feeling of uplift if they were sticking in their Metropolitan Museum of Art stickers instead watching "Scooby Doo" on Saturday morning . . . or even *while* watching "Scooby Doo."

Fast forward a year. I got to go on a business trip to Paris, and I decided to take the kids with me and expose them to some cultural enrichment. This meant, among other things, a trip to the Louvre, which I was frankly a little nervous about. Two preadolescent kids in a museum? It's the stuff of situation comedy. But Kyle and Rhett were awestruck . . . and more than awestruck. Standing in front of paintings, they were saying things like:

"Look! It's a Monet!"

"Yes, and it's the only one where he painted clouds like that."

"Here's a Degas—that's the one where he started to—"

The rest of their words are lost in time, but I still hear the excitement and enthusiam in their voices. The words are lost in time . . . and in the tears that rolled down my cheeks.

Summer Camps

One focused way that you can assure that your children get some of the enrichment you want for them is in summer camp. There are general purpose camps and there are specialized camps, focusing on the arts, computer skills, sports, weight loss, remedial study skills, sailing . . . almost anything your child has a special interest in.

Camp is a summer activity, and summer is for fun, but camp is an expense, part of your investment in your child's future, so you want to see a return on investment from it. You want your child to come back from camp having gained something.

What's an appropriate goal to set? If you expect your child to go to six or eight weeks of summer camp and come back with a mastery of C++ programming language, or ready to audition for the Metropolitan Opera, or get a basketball scholarship to Duke, you're going to be disappointed. And you're probably going to communicate that disappointment to your child: something you really don't want to do. So what should you expect?

Richard C. Kennedy and Michael Kimball, in *Choosing the Right Camp*, suggest that although a summer camp ought to be a learning experience, "the best camps . . . employ a learning system that might at first seem to be upside down . . . or at least contrary to the traditional view of what is most important and what is least important about learning."

Kennedy and Kimball propose that the quality of the camp experience is not in the amount of knowledge your child comes home with—the short time your child spends at a camp is just not enough for amassing a significant amount of knowledge. Instead, they say, you can expect your child to develop *skills*, which they describe as "everything from how to make friends to tying knots, from staying clean to hitting a backhand shot at tennis." But most of all, they suggest, camp can make a difference in a camper's *attitude*: "how to be considerate of other people, how to be a good sport, how to sustain a high degree of effort in order to achieve a worthy goal. In the best of camps, staff members are carefully chosen not only for their expertise in a particular field but, more important, for their abilities as mentors—role models."

Of course, the development of attitude and skills are a strong underpinning for the acquisition of knowledge. If your child is going to a general purpose camp where there's a little of everything, the "enrichment of its campers by bringing about measurable changes in their attitudes" is a worthy goal. If it's a camp that specializes in something your child is already pursuing, or plans to pursue in depth, then attitude and skills can really be at the service of knowledge.

Don't forget, also, that the childhood and teenage years are a time for exploration. A drama camp for a high school sophomore doesn't mean you're committing your child to the uncertain world of the stage, but he may learn something about carrying himself, and some important insights into human nature that can make a difference to a future business executive, or a doctor explaining something to a sick child. A basketball camp doesn't have to mean she's putting all her hopes into an athletic scholarship; it can be the basis for self-discipline and leadership in a wide range of careers.

Some Factors to Consider in Choosing a Camp: Focus

Does my child have a special interest, or would a general purpose camp work better?	
If a special interest, what is it?	

Location

Is camp near enough to drive to?	
Is camp near public transportation? Will someone pick your child up from train/bus/plane?	
Is camp safe and well maintained?	
Is camp in a locale appropriate for your child's interests?	

Characteristics

Is the camp small enough that your child will get enough individual attention?	
Is the camp co-ed or same sex?	
Does the camp have regional and ethnic diversity?	
Does the camp have a good representation of children your child's age?	
Will a sufficient core group of kids be there for the same length of time as your child?	

Staff and Program

What are the background and qualifications of the director, counselors and staff? Are you satisfied with them?	
Are the facilities and equipment up-to-date and well maintained?	
Does the camp have a clear stated philosophy and goals for its campers?	

(continued on next page)

Is the program appropriate for the age of your child?	
Are the medical facilities and staff adequate?	
Is there a hospital nearby?	
Are the kitchen and dining facilities adequate?	
For a specialized camp: Will there be direct instruction or supervision by highly qualified people?	

Cost

Tuition	
Extra fees—what are they for?	
Transportation	
Spending money	
Total	

Finally, and this is a judgment call, an important one—do you feel as though you'll be getting your money's worth?

You're dealing here with widely varying expenses, and with variable expenses. You're dealing with wants rather than needs. So when you put these figures into your consolidation worksheet, make sure you use a particularly light pencil, so you can alter them, if need be, to fit the realities of your budget.

Time Line 6

	1996	1997	1998	1999	2000	2001	2002	2003
Total current expenses								
Total baby expenses								
Total child care expenses								
Total shelter expenses (ongoing)								
Total enrichment expenses								
TOTAL EXPENSES								
TOTAL INCOME								
TOTAL SAVINGS								
Cash outlay from savings: shelter								
Cash outlay from savings: college								
NET SAVINGS								
TARGET SAVINGS								
CLOSENESS TO SAVINGS GOAL +/-								

2004	2005	2006	2007	2008	2009	2010	2011	2012	2013

8

Big Stuff and Being Prepared for It

Managing your money would be a lot simpler if nothing out of the ordinary ever happened in your life. But your life would be a whole lot duller. Susan Sarandon tells Winona Ryder, in one of the most moving scenes in *Little Women*, "My Jo, you have such extraordinary gifts—how could you ever expect to live an ordinary life?"

We all have extraordinary gifts, from special interests and abilities to the gift for loving our children, and none of our lives are ordinary. They have family and religious occasions, rites of passage like weddings and bar Mitzvahs and christenings, and none of these occasions are ever even remotely ordinary, because they involve our hearts. But they cost money, and they have to be figured into the budget somehow, as *variable expenses*—they can't cost any more than you have in your budget to pay for them.

Big expenses can also include medical/dental procedures that are elective or cosmetic, and therefore don't fall under your health insurance policy. These can include nose jobs or

214

braces, certain types of counseling, perhaps even certain types of summer camps, like a weight-loss camp or a remedial study habits camp.

Finally, big expenses can include enrichment items that have outgrown your budget for enrichment and moved into the category of "magnificent obsession." I'm talking about things like the Lhasa apso that Jennie has bred and trained and is now ready to compete in the Westminster Kennel Club dog show. Or the folk dance troupe Sean joined in the fourth grade that was so cute when it won a local talent show the next year, and made you so proud when it won the all-state contest sponsored by the Ancient Order of Hibernians, and now they've been invited to go over to Ireland for the all-Ireland folk dance festival (this actually happened to a family that Tad knew). Or the science project that Erin has gotten so involved in that might win her a college scholarship, or even a valuable patent, if she can just get that new transformer. . . .

The kids can pay for some of this themselves, or you can help them out through brains rather than cash: Ingenuity will get you through times of no money better than money will get you through times of no ingenuity. My sisters and I were mad about horses when we were kids. I pursued it by entering horse shows, even winning some ribbons. It's an interest that has actually helped me in the business world as an interest in common that enabled me to get to know people and clinch deals on more than one occasion. Beyond that, it has given me deep, soul-satisfying pleasure. We weren't a family that could afford a stable of horses, but we paid for our riding lessons by cleaning out a local stable, and eventually, due to an ingenious stategy on the part of my parents, we had our own horses—at least for part of the year.

My parents contacted a local summer camp that advertised riding as an activity and asked them what they did with their horses in the winter. The answer was, "Gosh, we don't know . . . different things . . . you got any ideas?"

My parents had an excellent idea, for three of the horses. We made an agreement with the horse farm where we worked. They had the extra space, and they let us stable the horses there, as long as we paid for their feed. So all winter, we had our own horses.

But sometimes, a magnificent obsession can suddenly throw off a big expense—a wonderful opportunity, or something that would be a wonderful opportunity if you could only manage to scrape up the bucks for it. That's more of the unpredictable Big Stuff—you don't know when it will happen, or how much it's going to cost, but the odds are that it will come up at some time or another.

You should prepare for the Big Stuff in two different ways:

First, prepare for the stuff you know is going to happen by identifying it, prioritizing it, and budgeting for it.

Second, prepare for the stuff that you don't know is going to happen by creating a contingency fund.

You can handle the first part in two different ways. As I said, these are variable expenses, a small (although significant) subcategory of your total expense picture. So I believe you should deal with this issue in the way that's most comfortable to you.

If you want to start out with a dream list, the way you did in the beginning of the book, you can do that. Fantasize your way through all the Big Stuff you'd like your kids to have, then start putting price tags on it, and then start cutting back.

Or if you'd rather not, at this point, be faced with contemplating a whole bunch of good stuff you won't ever be able to spend your money on, you can approach it from the reverse angle. Make your list, then estimate a total budget for Big Stuff, and then put your list into the budget according to the percentage of the total you're going to spend on each.

In either case, start out the same way.

For each item, mark your choice on the basis of how important it is to fulfill your wish in this area, then (for couples) add the numbers together to come up with a total. You remember the scale:

0 = I really don't want this
1 = I never think about it
2 = I could be talked into it
3 = I have moderate interest
4 = I would really like this
5 = I don't see how I could live without it

The difference between the way you'll apply this scale here and the way you applied it to something like buying a house is that there are no absolutes. A zero on one partner's list doesn't rule something out, a five doesn't make it mandatory. This stuff is important, but it's not *as* important.

Big Stuff Dream List

Item	Partner 1	Partner 2	Total
Big celebrations/parties			
Wedding			
Engagement party			
Bridal shower			
Bar/bas mitzvah			
College graduation			
High school graduation			
Christening			
First communion			

(continued on next page)

ITEM	PARTNER 1	PARTNER 2	TOTAL
BIG CELEBRATIONS/PARTIES			
Senior prom			
Sweet sixteen			
Other			

For each of the parties, figure out what you want and how much it will cost. Price each item out at today's prices, and then extrapolate it into the future. Here's a way of estimating the rise in price—just double the price for events that will happen 8–12 years in the future, triple the price for events 13–17 years in the future, and quadruple the price for events 18–22 years in the future.

Big Celebrations/Parties

EVENT_____CHILD_____			
ITEM	**COST**	**YEARS IN FUTURE**	**ESTIMATED COST**
Catering			
for ____ people			
for ____ people			
for ____ people			

(continued on next page

Item	Cost	Years in future	Estimated cost
Flowers			
Music			
Photographer			
Transportation			
Gift			
Location			
Cost of ceremony			
Other			
Total			

Create one of these "Parties" worksheets for every event that's important to you, and total up how much you'd be spending for each child. Don't forget, these are just the expenses that are connected to predictable family ceremonies. They don't include "magnificent obsessions." As these come along, you'll have to make space for them in the budget—which may mean paring other things back.

Don't forget about *opportunity cost*—money you spend on one event is money that's not going to be there for another.

You may not want to go into such detail on a Big Stuff dream list. There are some dreams we don't want to dream in such detail if they have a low priority for coming true. You may not want to know just how much it would be fun to spend. The alternative is simply to figure out how much money you're going to have available for Big Stuff, divide it by the number of kids you have, and then apportion out what percentage of each child's share goes for what.

I recommend that no more than 10 percent of total savings be allotted to Big Stuff.

And remember—a good definition of Big Stuff is: *stuff you should not go into debt for.*

Wherever you start from, eventually you're going to have to come face to face with reality, and a budget. You can always work within a budget, if you set your mind to it. Not long ago, I was asked to help a family who had appeared on the Oprah Winfrey show (details slightly changed here). They were out of control. They knew they were spending too much, but they didn't know if they could stop.

Their daughter's wedding threatened to be the breaking point. The parents knew they could be seriously hurt by over-spending, but Alessia, their daughter, simply couldn't imagine holding back on anything.

"It's my *wedding!*" was her entire argument, and since that really isn't an argument, there was no answer to it.

She had started by buying a $1,000 dress.

That was when Oprah asked me to step in. I talked to Alessia's parents and figured out what they could actually afford. It was $5,000, total. That meant that there was $4,000 left over after the dress, and the spree had to be nipped in the bud quickly.

I went over the numbers with Alessia, replacing her parents' vague fears with hard facts. Then we sat down to do the planning. Alessia pouted, at first, but then she said, hesitantly, "Well . . . I know where I can get a pair of shoes wholesale, for thirty-five dollars."

She smiled shyly. I knew the look—the first realization of the empowerment that comes from knowing you can control your spending, that it doesn't have to control you.

We started researching costs. Alessia and her fiancé are from Oklahoma, but she discovered that if they got married in Las Vegas, the cost of everything would be much lower.

We stuck with it, and we put together a $5,000 wedding that Alessia was proud of.

Alessia's Wedding

Gown	$1,000
Shoes	$35
4 hotel rooms	$200
Air fare	$1,000
Wedding banquet	$900
Flowers	$200
Music	$300
Rehearsal dinner	$120
Cake	$100
Photographer/video	$600
Invitations	$200
Tips	$100
TOTAL	$4,755

With $250 left over for incidentals, they were in under budget.

Elective Medical/Dental/Counseling Expenses

You can use your family histories to anticipate some of these costs. If you had braces, a nose job, or any other elective process, then there's a good chance your children will have the same conditions, heredity being what it is. So, while these expenses make up another category that you can't predict with any certainty, you can at least identify tendencies and be aware of them. Start by making a list of things you needed:

Family History

ITEM	PARTNER 1 — HISTORY	PARTNER 2 — HISTORY
Dental		
Elective medical		
Counseling		
Remedial education		

Apportioning Big Stuff Expenses

There are a lot of judgment calls here, and they're important judgment calls. Everything in this chapter is a part of Big Stuff. They're large expenses. You know you're going to have some of them. You don't know exactly which ones, and you don't know exactly when.

Not all Big Stuff is equal, though. Some of it is Want, and some of it is Need. Within the Want category, some of it is High-Priority Want, and some of it is much lower priority. Among the Needs and the High-Priority Wants, there can be Fixed and Variable expenses.

In other words, a big wedding might be a High-Priority Want—if you are flat broke, you might not be able to do it, but it will have tremendous meaning for not only your daughter, but everyone in your family. A Sweet Sixteen party might be a much lower priority Want. A bar mitzvah might be a Need, if your family is religiously observant. But all three of those occasions are Variable expenses.

On the other hand, some Big Stuff items may be both Needs and Fixed expenses. Those braces on your child's teeth may be absolutely necessary to correct a serious problem. Divorce or a family tragedy may make counseling a Need; a learning disability may require special therapy.

These are not only Needs, not only Fixed expenses, they are also family problems, not individual expenses. If one of your children has one of these needs, it must be understood that everyone in the family rallies around to help. This expense comes from the total Big Stuff budget, not just from that individual child's share.

These items can start moving over into an area where Big Stuff may start sounding like too frivolous a name for them—and clearly, if they're both Needs and Fixed expenses, then you may have to go into debt for them.

Windfalls

There's Big Stuff that you spend . . . and there's also Big Stuff that you get.

Very few readers of this book are going to win the lottery. As someone who believes in a carefully planned investment strategy, I don't even recommend that you play it.

But there are other kinds of windfalls: An inheritance is one of the most common. At certain times in your life, you're likely to come into the possession of sums of money—even large sums—that are over and above what you're budgeting with. What do you with them?

Well, here's my advice, and it's simple:

Put 40–45% into your kids' college fund.
Put 40–45% into your retirement fund.
Put the rest into your Big Stuff fund.

A Little Perspective

Alessia was able to put her wedding expenses in perspective. It wasn't easy, but she did it, and she felt better for doing it— she gained that empowerment that comes from not being a victim of your own finances.

But when I was looking for a way to put this concept of perspective into words, I found I couldn't do better than the words of my daughter, Kyle, in the speech she gave at her bas mitzvah. We didn't have the bas mitzvah in a big hall, with a DJ and a big party, because there was something more important that Kyle wanted to do that day: include her great-grandmother, homebound by illness, in the festivities. Here's a part of what Kyle said:

Hi, today's my bas mitzvah, but does anyone actually know what the word *bas mitzvah* means? Does it mean graduation from Hebrew school? No! Does it mean becoming a woman? Not really. Does it mean a party with a DJ? Not at all! *Bas* means daughter, *Mitzvah* means commandments. So the word *bas mitzvah* means "daughter of commandments." A girl becomes bas mitzvah'd the day she turns twelve on the Hebrew calendar, whether she has a party or not, and even if she doesn't give a big speech, or a Rabbi wasn't there, or no one was there. H——— says that when a girl turns twelve, she is mature enough to be responsible to observe the Mitzvahs. . . .

This day is special. And what's special about today is what's special about Judaism. That is the *family*. The family is the center of Jewish life.

I'm so lucky to be here today with four generations of family. How many kids have great-grandmothers? I'm also lucky to be part of an American Jewish family. The Godfrey side of the family goes back eleven generations in the United States. Our Judaism has been preserved.

Some people think that in order to be religious, you have to go to Temple and you have to be bas mitzvah'd in Temple. It is special for Jews to have temples. That is a mitzvah. But that is not the heart of Judaism—the home is the heart. Jews can be Jews and even religious without temples.

In America, being bas mitzvah'd has turned into having a great big party, and ending your Jewish education. The way it's really supposed to be is, once you turn twelve you become more responsible for keeping the Mitzvahs.

Today as we celebrate my bas mitzvah, the most important thing is the family. That's why you're all here! So if Granny Jewel couldn't come to the bas mitzvah, we'd bring the bas mitzvah to Granny Jewel.

Time Line 7

	1996	1997	1998	1999	2000	2001	2002	2003
Total current expenses								
Total baby expenses								
Total child care expenses								
Total shelter expenses (ongoing)								
Total enrichment expenses								
TOTAL ANTICIPATED EXPENSES								
Total unexpected expenses								
TOTAL INCOME								
TOTAL SAVINGS								
Cash outlay from savings: shelter								
Cash outlay from savings: college								
Windfall savings								
NET SAVINGS								
TARGET SAVINGS								
CLOSENESS TO SAVINGS GOAL +/-								

2004	2005	2006	2007	2008	2009	2010	2011	2012	2013

9

Investing

You're going to go through a period of your life where your
earning potential is healthy and growing, and you're going to
go through periods of your life when you'll have tremendous
financial demands made on you, and there simply will not be
enough money coming in to handle all those demands. Your
children's college years will be one of those periods; your
retirement will be another. If, as so many are doing today,
you've put off having children into your thirties or even your
forties, these two peaks of financial need will come danger-
ously close together.

The way to prepare for these exigencies is a careful financial strategy—a careful strategy of investment.

Rule One

Rule One is simple, and if you never explore any other financial strategy but just remember this rule, you'll be in pretty
good shape:

Start young.

Yes, it really is as simple as that. If you start investing when

you're young enough, and leave your investment to com-
pound, it will mount up. By the time you're older, and ready
to use it, you'll have a very sizable investment.

If you don't start investing until you're older, your money
simply is not going to do the same work for you.

How does this work out in practice? Well, take a look at the
following chart, and see what happens to $1,000 a year,
invested at a 10 percent rate of return, in a variety of scenarios.

In other words, your investment of $1,000 a year for ten
years, from ages 25–34, will have grown by 3,265 percent by
the time you reach age 65.

Your investment of $1,000 a year for thirty-one years, from
ages 35–65, will have grown by 552 percent by the time you
reach age 65.

Your investment of $2,000 a year for twenty-one years, from
ages 45–65, will have grown by 243 percent by the time you
reach age 65.

Your investment of $1,000 a year for forty-one years, from
ages 25–65, will have grown by 11,916 percent by the time you
reach age 65!!!!

The Rule of 72

Here's another worthwhile rule to remember when you're trying to visualize the concept of saving and investing money.
The rate of return on your investment, divided into 72, equals
the number of years it will take to double your investment. In
other words, if your investments are making 9 percent interest, then divide 72 by nine—you'll have doubled your original
investment in eight years.

Investment Objectives

Putting money aside—and putting it aside early—is the cor-
nerstone of any investment program. Beyond that, there's the

Table 8: Return on $1,000 a Year (or More)

AGE	INV.	RET.	INV.	RET.	INV.	RET.	INV.	RET.	INV.	RET.
25	$1,000	$1,100					$1,000	$1,100		
26	1,000	2,310					1,000	2,310		
27	1,000	3,640					1,000	3,640		
28	1,000	5,110					1,000	5,110		
29	1,000	6,720					1,000	6,720		
30	1,000	8,490					1,000	8,490		
31	1,000	10,440					1,000	10,440		
32	1,000	12,580					1,000	12,580		
33	1,000	14,940					1,000	14,940		
34	1,000	17,530					1,000	17,530		

(continued on next page)

AGE	INV.	RET.	INV.	RET.	INV.	RET.	INV.	RET.	INV.	RET.
35		19,280	1,000	1,100			1,000	20,380		
36		21,210	1,000	2,310			1,000	23,620		
37		23,330	1,000	3,640			1,000	26,970		
38		25,670	1,000	5,110			1,000	30,770		
39		28,230	1,000	6,720			1,000	34,950		
40		31,060	1,000	8,490			1,000	39,540		
41		34,160	1,000	10,440			1,000	44,600		
42		37,580	1,000	12,580			1,000	50,160		
43		41,340	1,000	14,940			1,000	56,270		
44		46,470	1,000	17,530			1,000	63,000		

(continued on next page)

AGE	INV.	RET.	INV.	RET.	INV.	RET.	INV.	RET.	INV.	RET.
45		50,020	1,000	19,280	2,000	2,200	1,000	70,400	5,000	5,500
46		55,020	1,000	23,520	2,000	4,620	1,000	78,540	5,000	11,550
47		69,529	1,000	26,970	2,000	7,280	1,000	87,500	5,000	15,210
48		66,570	1,000	30,770	2,000	10,210	1,000	97,350	5,000	25,530
49		73,230	1,000	34,950	2,000	13,430	1,000	108,180	5,000	33,580
50		80,560	1,000	39,540	2,000	16,970	1,000	120,100	5,000	42,440
51		88,610	1,000	44,600	2,000	20,870	1,000	133,210	5,000	52,180
52		97,470	1,000	50,160	2,000	25,160	1,000	147,630	5,000	62,900
53		107,220	1,000	56,270	2,000	29,870	1,000	163,490	5,000	74,690
54		117,940	1,000	63,000	2,000	35,060	1,000	180,940	5,000	87,660

(continued on next page)

Age	Inv.	Ret.	Inv.	Ret.	Inv.	Ret.	Inv.	Ret.	Inv.	Ret.	Inv.	Ret.
55		129,740	1,000	70,400	2,000	40,770	1,000	200,140	5,000	101,920		
56		142,710	1,000	78,540	2,000	47,050	1,000	221,250	5,000	117,610		
57		156,980	1,000	87,500	2,000	53,950	1,000	244,480	5,000	134,870		
58		172,680	1,000	97,350	2,000	61,500	1,000	270,020	5,000	153,860		
59		189,950	1,000	108,180	2,000	69,900	1,000	298,130	5,000	174,750		
60		208,940	1,000	120,100	2,000	79,090	1,000	329,040	5,000	197,720		
61		229,830	1,000	133,210	2,000	89,200	1,000	363,040	5,000	223,000		
62		262,800	1,000	147,630	2,000	100,320	1,000	400,450	5,000	250,800		
63		278,100	1,000	163,490	2,000	112,550	1,000	441,590	5,000	281,370		
64		305,910	1,000	180,940	2,000	126,000	1,000	486,850	5,000	315,010		
65		336,500	1,000	200,140	2,000	140,810	1,000	536,640	5,000	352,010		
Total	$10,000	$336,500	$31,000	$200,140	$42,000	$140,810	$41,000	$536,640	$105,000	$352,010		

question of an investment strategy, and to determine the best strategy for you, you have to figure out your *objectives*—what are you going to need money for, and when are you going to need it?

There are three basic investment objectives: *keeping your principal safe; keeping a regular flow of money coming in;* and *making more money.*

Keeping your principal safe: When you're saving for something specific in the future (for example, college or retirement) or to prepare for expensive eventualities (for example, illness or death), you'll want to make sure that you have your money in investments that will not diminish, even if the economy falters and price levels fall—safe, conservative investments.

It's important that these investments play a part in your overall investment strategy, because the money has to be there for those unavoidable expenses.

The problem is, keeping your principal safe is bound to mean that you're lowering your potential for profit and income. The safest investments are going to have the least potential for an upside; there's no way around that.

Keeping money coming in: When you're getting near retirement, you'll be thinking about how much your investments yield, because after your salary stops, that yield is going to be your principal income. You calculate yield by dividing the annual return by the cost of the investment.

There's a risk factor in high-yield investments: generally speaking, the higher the yield, the more unsafe the principal. On the other hand, there's a less obvious, but very real, risk in safer, low-income investments. You're surer of being able to count on a regular flow of income, but it's possible that inflation can make the purchasing power of that income decline, so that over time you'll end up with an actual loss of purchasing power.

Making more money: If you didn't have be concerned with getting your hands on a certain amount of money at a certain time, you could invest for *growth*—you could put your money into investments that are riskier. I don't mean to suggest you should be reckless, taking irresponsible risks. But there are many responsible investments that carry a reasonable level of risk. That means that, in the long run, these investments are a very good strategy for increasing your capital. But you have to be prepared for riding out rough times.

If you're going to need to cash in those investments in ten years, and the economy is in a recession in ten years, then they may turn out to be bad investments. But if you can afford to hold on to your investments through that recession, then you can let them go on making money for you in the long term. If you want your money to be worth more for you in that long term, you have to have some growth investments.

So, all three of these investment strategies have their advantages and disadvantages. A well-designed investment strategy should make some use of all three.

Investment Principles

There is, of course, no single master plan for a well-designed investment strategy. It has to be tailored to your own needs. As you get ready to design your own strategy, here are a few investment principles you need to understand.

Goal Orientation. You can't design a strategy to reach your goals until you've defined what those goals are. And you aren't likely to reach those goals unless you have two things: the discipline to stick to your plans and the flexibility to adjust them when economic and life changes dictate an adjustment.

Dollar Cost Averaging. If you're investing for long-term need, like a college fund, you want to make sure that your money keeps growing, and that you don't get hurt. Since there's always some risk in any investment, it's important that you make sure the risk is minimized.

The stock market, over this century, has been generally a good investment. But if you try to play it too aggressively, it can backfire on you. Everyone wants to buy low and sell high, but if you try too hard to hit the market at the precise best moment, it can backfire on you.

Dollar cost averaging is a good alternative. That means investing small amounts over a regular period of time, rather than trying to outguess the market. If you invest, say, $100 every month, no matter how the stock or mutual fund market is doing, or how high or low interest rates have gone, this gives you the following advantages:

You wind up buying more shares when prices are low, and fewer when prices are high. Since you're investing a fixed amount periodically and not buying a certain number of shares, you're leveling out your average cost per share, over time.

This technique is better for buying no-load mutual funds than individual stocks, because you don't have to keep paying commissions.

You can also apply roughly the same principle to stocks with dividend reinvestments (DRIPS). In these plans, the shareholder automatically reinvests dividends in more shares of the company's stock. Companies generally encourage this: Some will absorb most or all of your brokerage fees, and some will discount the stock price.

Diversification. One danger of investing is committing too large an amount to just one kind of investment. That's like putting all your eggs in one basket: If that investment drops dramatically, you could be crippled by it, and it could take you years to recover. If you need to make sure that your desired goal is met at a certain time—say, when your child is ready for college—well, you just can't afford that.

If you spread your risk around by putting your assets into several categories of investments—stocks, bonds, money markets, etc.—you have a cushion against being hurt if one investment vehicle performs badly.

Laddering. This basically means buying investment vehicles, such as bonds or CDs, that have different lengths of time to maturity as a hedge against being caught with all your investments maturing at one time, when interest rates may be unfavorable.

Liquidity. An investment is liquid to the extent that you can cash it in quickly, without taking a loss. This is a relative term—some investments are more liquid than others.

This is another area where you need balance, because again there's a trade-off—your growth investments, those investments that will make you the most money in the long run, are generally the least liquid.

Income Tax Deferral. If income tax on an investment is deferred, that means you still have to pay it, but you don't have to pay it until later—sometimes many years later.

We've talked about the time value of money. Well, that concept comes into play here. If you have two investments that are equal in all other respects, but one of them has deferred income tax, then you have that extra money—the taxes that you can put off paying—working for you.

Choosing an Investment Advisor

If you've got your basic living expenses covered—housing, insurance, and a cash reserve fund for emergencies—then it's time to start thinking about some form of savings or investment plan.

Acquiring and managing investments takes more than just money—it also takes time and know-how. You might be able to manage all of your investments by yourself, but the knowledge you'd need is so specialized that you might well be better off entrusting your portfolio to a professional. Even so, the more you know yourself, the better able you will be to select a financial advisor you can trust.

The following people can advise you on investing. If licensed, they can also make investments for you:

Lawyers
CPAs
Financial consultants
Insurance brokers
Bank financial planners
Discount brokers

Certified Financial Planners

Financial planners can be *fee-only planners,* who charge an hourly or a flat fee for consultation with you, *commission-only planners,* who take a commission on sales of investment products, and *fee and commission planners,* who receive payments on a combination of both.

Is one better than another? Not necessarily. Commission rates may vary, but they're so heavily regulated that it's not a big deal; if you spend a lot of time looking for discount rates, the amount of money you'll save over the long run will be minimal. It's more important to find an advisor who satisfies you in other ways.

Still, it's a good idea to get a written estimate of what services you can expect for what price.

The most common way of finding an investment advisor is word of mouth—talk to friends and family, find out who they use, how satisfied they are, and what it is that makes them satisfied.

When I did a regular radio talk show, I used to have my 90-year-old grandmother on as a guest once a week because, in addition to being my best friend, Grandma Jewel has more common sense on just about every subject in the world than anyone I know. She was on the show one day when a listener called in with the question, How do you find the right financial advisor? Grandma Jewel's answer: "The same way you find anything else. Just ask the girls down at the beauty parlor!"

There are also organizations that represent financial planners who have taken courses and passed examinations in such fields as wills, trusts, investments, taxes, home ownership, and life and health insurance. Investment advisors can be certified by these organizations, but there are no real regulations in most states for the financial planning industry.

Once you've gotten a list of potential investment advisors, you can start interviewing a few. You'll want to know their background, including credentials. You'll want to know if they have skills, expertise, and philosophical outlook to fill your specific needs. If you want to invest conservatively, you don't want a daring buccaneer; by the same token, if you want to invest aggressively and take some risks, you don't want someone who is overcautious. You'll want to know what kind of services the company offers.

Very important, if you're young and a new investor, especially if you're starting with a modest amount of money, you want an advisor who will sit down and spend some time with you. If you get someone who's just going to plug you into a computer model, or who won't return your phone calls because he's spending all his time with his big bucks investors, find someone new.

You have a right to expect this, and you have a right to expect not to be intimidated.

It's strange . . . in many ways money is the last social frontier, the last taboo. In the past twenty years, we've learned—especially women—not to be intimidated by doctors. We've learned that you don't just have to nod timidly and accept everything a doctor says; today, we wouldn't think of leaving a doctor's office without asking the purpose of the treatment, and the cost of treatment, and alternative courses of treatment. But we may very well still find ourselves nodding silently at a financial consultant, grinning foolishly, feeling too ignorant—and too afraid to show our ignorance—to ask any questions at all. This has got to change.

You should also be careful of planners who use high-pressure tactics, promise incredibly high rates of return, or try to convince you to sign on the dotted line without taking some time to think it over.

You have a right to change if you decide that your financial planner isn't giving you the service, or the results, you're looking for. If you sent your best suit to the cleaners and it came back with spots on it, you wouldn't keep going to that cleaner, would you?

Next, make sure you know what you have: a complete picture of your assets, liabilities, and cash flow. Here are some worksheets to help you create that picture.

Assets

ASSET	CURRENT VALUE		
	PARTNER 1	PARTNER 2	TOTAL
Checking accounts			
Savings accounts			
Money market accounts/funds			
Certificates of deposit			
IRA accounts			
Keogh accounts			
Pension/profit-sharing accounts			
Life insurance cash values			

(continued on next page)

ASSET	CURRENT VALUE		
	PARTNER 1	PARTNER 2	TOTAL
Annuities			
Bonds (government)			
Bonds (corporate)			
Mutual funds			
Stocks			
Other securities			
Receivables (money owed you)			
Home			
Other real estate			
Automobiles			
Collectibles			

(continued on next page)

ASSET	CURRENT VALUE		
	PARTNER 1	PARTNER 2	TOTAL
Other personal property			
Household furnishings			
Jewelry			
TOTAL ASSETS			

Liabilities

LIABILITY	CURRENT VALUE		
	PARTNER 1	PARTNER 2	TOTAL
Home mortgage			
Other mortgages			
Auto loans			
Credit card balances			
Installment accounts			
Contracts/money borrowed			
Income taxes			
Pledges			
Other			
TOTAL LIABILITIES			

Net Worth

NET WORTH (Assets minus liabilities)			

Cash Flow—Income

PERIOD: TO			
INCOME	PARTNER 1	PARTNER 2	TOTAL
Salary/wages			
Commissions			
Bonuses			
Interest/dividends			
Social security			
Retirement plans			
Reimbursement/refunds			
Sale of investments			
Other			
TOTAL INCOME			

Cash Flow—Expenses

PERIOD:_____ TO_____			
EXPENSE	**PARTNER 1**	**PARTNER 2**	**TOTAL**
Savings			
Income taxes			
Property taxes			
Insurance			
Debt payments			
Mortgage/rent			
Utilities			
Child care			
Transportation:			

(continued on next page)

INCOME	PARTNER 1	PARTNER 2	TOTAL
Food/supermarket items			
Restaurants			
Recreation			
Holiday Expenses			
Gifts			
Education/enrichment			
Clothing			
Camp			
Other			
TOTAL EXPENSES			

Investment Risks

You know that all investments have risks, some greater than others. And you know that you have to assess how much risk you can tolerate when you're devising an investment strategy. You should also know what kinds of risks are associated with buying securities. There are four major risks:

Business risk: When you invest in a company, either by lending to it (buying bonds) or by purchasing equity in it (buying stocks), you're taking the risk that the company may not be sound. Since bondholders have to be paid off first by a troubled company, there is less business risk in buying bonds.

Market risk: This is the risk that the market value, particularly of a stock, can go down. Dollar cost averaging is a good way of reducing market risk.

Rate risk: This is a risk associated with bonds or any interest-bearing instrument. If the interest rate is down when your bond matures, this can cost you. And if interest rates go down, your bond may be called. Laddering is a good way of reducing rate risk, so all your money does not mature at the same time.

Purchasing power risk: If your capital is growing because you've been saving and investing your money, it's not necessarily growing as fast as you think. That's because inflation grows, too, and that decreases the purchasing power of each dollar. If your investments are too conservative, there's even a risk that you could fall behind inflation.

How much of your dollar does inflation eat up? Here's a look at the Consumer Price Index from 1967 to 1993, as compiled by the U.S. Bureau of Labor Statistics. The Consumer Price Index is the government's statistical measure of the changes in the price of goods and services bought by urban wage earners and clerical workers, which makes it the most common standard used to measure the rate of inflation.

Table 9: Inflation and the Dollar—1967–1993

YEAR	INDEX	% INCREASE	PURCHASING POWER OF THE DOLLAR
1967	100.0	—	$1.00
1968	104.2	4.2%	.96
1969	109.8	5.4%	.91
1970	116.3	5.9%	.86
1971	121.3	4.3%	.82
1972	125.3	3.3%	.80
1973	133.1	6.2%	.75
1974	147.7	11.0%	.68
1975	161.2	9.1%	.62
1976	170.5	5.8%	.59
1977	181.5	6.5%	.55
1978	195.4	7.7%	.51
1979	217.4	11.3%	.46
1980	246.8	13.5%	.41
1981	272.4	10.4%	.37
1982	290.6	6.7%	.34
1983	301.5	3.8%	.33

(continued on next page)

YEAR	INDEX	% INCREASE	PURCHASING POWER OF THE DOLLAR
1984	312.2	3.5%	.32
1985	323.4	3.6%	.31
1986	325.7	0.7%	.31
1987	340.2	4.4%	.29
1988	357.9	5.2%	.28
1989	371.1	3.7%	.27
1990	399.4	7.6%	.25
1991	404.7	1.3%	.25
1992	416.3	2.9%	.24
1993	423.1	1.6%	.24

Does this mean that the purchasing power of your dollar is shrinking so rapidly, you're better off running out and spending it right now? How does the time value of money enter into this?

Well, let's compare the figures here with the figures in Table 8: Return on $1,000 a Year (or More). If our 25-year-old from Table 8 had started saving her $1,000 a year for ten years in 1967, then by 1993 her $10,000 would have turned into $97,470. If her purchasing power in 1967 dollars is down to 24 cents, then it's still worth $23,392.80—she can still buy more than twice, in goods and services, than she could then.

Let's suppose our saver is an older gent, so he's reaching retirement in 1993. That means he started saving in 1953 (and don't forget we're supposing a conservative investor here, satisfied with a steady 10 percent over the forty years of his investment). In 1967, his nest egg is worth $23,330. In 1995, it's worth $336,500—or $80,760 in 1967 dollars.

Stocks and Bonds—What's the Difference?

When you buy a stock, you're investing in the company itself, actually buying a piece of the company, and that stock will continue to exist for as long as the company is in existence, or until you sell it. When you buy a bond, you're lending money to the company, and it will continue to earn interest for you until it matures, for as long as the company is in existence, or until you sell it.

If the company goes bankrupt, your claim as a bondholder comes before the interests of a stockholder, because you're a creditor rather than a part owner.

Some Other Things You Should Know About Bonds

A *call* on a bond comes when the bond issuer decides it wants to retire a debt, and it can come as an unpleasant surprise. It means that you lose out on interest payments. That works like this: If you have a $1,000 bond that pays 6 percent, maturing in twenty years, then every year you get 6 percent interest, or $60. Assuming you don't reinvest any of it, at the end of the twenty years you've gotten $1,200 in interest payments, and then your original $1,000 is returned to you. If the bond is called at the end of ten years, you get your $1,000 returned to you, but you've only made $600 in interest. Of course, you can turn around and buy another $1,000 bond, but if interest rates are lower, you'll lose on the deal—and normally, calls are made in times of low interest, since those are the times when retiring a debt becomes an attractive proposition for the issuer.

Many bondholders are protected from calls for at least ten years after a bond is issued, and most bonds are called at a premium, but you should still find out from your broker whether you're at risk on any existing or contemplated investments.

You can check the ratings of bonds. Whenever you give your money to an organization of folks who promise they'll take it, use it, and give it back to you with interest, there are always two possibilities: first, that they'll do exactly what they've promised; second, that for one reason or another, they won't. To minimize your risk on the bond market, you should only buy quality, high-grade bonds. How do you know what grade the bond you're considering is? There are two companies that rate them: Moody's Investment Service and Standard and Poor's. Both are reliable; their ratings run from AAA (Moody's) or Aaa (S&P), which mean Best Quality, to C, which is the lowest grade, or D, which means the company is in default.

I would not recommend that you, as an individual investor, consider a bond rated any lower than A.

Here's a capsule guide to some of the major categories of investments.

Stocks

Table 10: Stocks

Vehicle	Stocks
Brief definition	Equity ownership shares in a corporation, represented by certificates for shares, that mean you have a claim on the corporation's earnings and assets. As a shareholder, you have a voice in the company's directorship, and can vote either in person or by proxy for its board of directors.

(continued on next page)

VEHICLE	STOCKS
Variations	*Preferred stocks* don't give you voting rights but do give you a prior claim on dividends—preferred stockholders must be paid before common stockholders.
Minimum purchase	One share
Holding period	None established
Tax status	As income, taxable gains
How to buy	Generally through a broker; some stocks can be bought directly.
What's good about them	Stocks have been, historically, the most profitable investment you can make.
What to watch for	Stocks are extremely volatile. You can reduce your risk by knowing—or making sure your broker knows—all elements of business, profitability. management and marketplace factors, and by making prudent, disciplined investments. But there will always be risk.

Here's a fun tip about stocks: This is isn't exactly another form of investment, and it shouldn't be the deciding factor in making an investment either, but there are certain investments that offer little extra bonuses—investments with perks, I call them. For example, if you own even one share of Disney stock, you get free admission to the Disney amusement parks.

Bonds

Table 11: Municipal Bonds

VEHICLE	MUNICIPAL BONDS *(Munis)*
Brief definition	A debt obligation that's issued either by a state or a municipality. You're loaning it money to support either general financial needs *(general obligation bonds)* or specific projects, like a bridge or a sewage treatment plant *(revenue bonds)*.
Variations	*Single-state municipal bond funds* include different bonds, all issued by agencies within one state, giving you the advantage of diversification. *Variable-rate option municipals* are really long-term municipal bonds, but because of the way they're structured, you don't have to keep your money in them for a long term. Their interest rates are adjusted to the current market rate, giving you the option, on a daily, weekly, monthly or yearly basis, of cashing in the bond and collecting what you paid for it.
Minimum investment	Usually $5000
Holding period	
Tax status	Generally tax-free on the Federal level. There's an incentive here to invest in our home state— if you live in the state where you purchase the fund, there are generally no state and local taxes either. This is a particularly strong selling point for single-state municipal bond funds.
How to buy	Generally through a broker

(continued on next page)

VEHICLE	MUNICIPAL BONDS *(Munis)*
What's good about them	Tax advantage Safety—munis are one of the safer bonds. Here are a couple of tips to make them even safer: *General obligation bonds* are even safer than revenue bonds, since the loan is to the whole municipality, not just to a specific project. *Insured municipal bonds* or *Unit Trusts* are backed by private insurance companies and are usually rated AAA or Aaa. Prices will still fluctuate, but the insurance companies will guarantee that you'll come out of the fund with the full payment of interest and principal (you'll pay for this guarantee, of course).
What to watch for	Munis *can* default if the state or city agency that issued the bond goes broke or defaults on its payments. This doesn't happen often, but it did in 1994, in Orange County, California. To minimize your chances of getting hurt this way, stay with high-rated, high-quality bonds.

Table 12: Zero-Coupon Bonds

VEHICLE	ZERO-COUPON BONDS *(zeros)*
Brief definition	Corporate or Treasury bonds for which all the interest is deferred until the bond reaches maturity; you're actually receiving zero money from interest during the life of the bond.
Variations	Some states issue a *baccalaureate bond,* a zero-coupon form of tax-free muni. They may include a bonus at maturity if your child decides to go to college in that state.
Minimum deposit	As little as $50

(continued on next page)

VEHICLE	ZERO-COUPON BONDS *(zeros)*
Holding period	Anywhere from 6 months to 30 years
Tax status	You must pay taxes on interest every year, even though you're not collecting any of that interest until the bond matures. There are ways you can avoid paying those taxes on "phantom" interest. You can buy your zero-coupon bonds for your IRA or Keogh plan, or some other tax-sheltered account; or you can invest in tax-free municipal zeros.
How to buy	Through your broker
What's good about them	Zeros sell at a deep discount, and you can get into them cheaply. You know what you're getting—a zero will mature into a specific sum, and you're told that sum when you buy it. You're not confronted every six months with the problem of re-investing your interest income at unpredictable rates. You just buy a zero and forget it, and somewhere down the line, you'll have a good deal more money than you started out with.
What to watch for	Prices of long-term zeros can fluctuate greatly. If you buy a zero and then interest rates go up, there's nothing you can do to cash in on that trend. Zeros can be called early. Watch out for brokers' markups. There's no standard, and every broker can charge different amounts, so shop around. Also, commissions can be steep if you make a minimum purchase.

Table 13: Treasuries

VEHICLE	TREASURIES
Brief definition	Debt obligations issued by the U.S. government
Variations	*Bills, notes* and *bonds* (see below)
Minimum deposit	Bills—$10,000 for the first. Subsequent bills can be purchased for $5,000 each. Notes—$5,000 when they mature in less than five years; $1,000 when they mature in more than five years. Bonds—$1,000
Holding period	Bills—3, 6 or 12 months Notes—2 to 10 years Bonds—minimum of 5 years
Tax status	Exempt from state and local, but not federal taxes.
How to buy*	You can buy Treasuries through any of the 12 Federal Reserve banks or 25 branch offices, or you can order them by mail, using forms that you can get from your local federal bank. You can also buy them from a commercial bank or broker. It's easier, but there is a commission that can cost $30–60, and it can lower your return. You can also buy them through certain mutual funds (which enables you, for a relatively small amount of money, to tap into a diversified portfolio of treasuries of different maturities.) Treasury bills are sold at auction by either *competitive* or *non-competitive* bid. Stick with non-competitive, which just means you'll pay the average rate at the auction.

(continued on next page)

VEHICLE	TREASURIES
Return on investment	T-bills are sold at a discount to their face value. Your return is the difference between what you invest and what you receive shortly after you invest. If one-year T-bills are paying 5%, you receive $500 back from a $10,000 investment, and your original $10,000 a year later. Thus, you're really getting your $500 as interest on $9,500, which means that your real rate of interest is 5.26%.
What's good about them	Treasuries are a US. government obligation, backed by the "full faith and credit" of the United States government. Although treasury bonds can theoretically be called five years before they come to maturity, in practice this just doesn't happen.
What to watch for	There's no credit risk, but there is a rate risk. You can lose money if you sell your security before it matures, and if interest rates have climbed. Here's how that works: If you hold a treasury bond worth $1000 which you bought at 6%, then every year the bond will pay you that 6%—$60 a year. If interest rates climb to 8%, then if you bought a $750 bond, that would pay you $60 a year. If you try to sell your $1000 bond at that point, it's worth will be figured by its interest—that is, it'll only be worth $750. You can balance out your interest rate risk by *laddering*, buying Treasuries that mature in a staggered pattern.

*For more information about buying Treasuries, write to:

Bureau of Public Debt
Dept. of Treasury
Washington, D.C. 20239

Table 14: Series EE Savings Bonds

Vehicle	Series EE Savings Bonds
Brief definition	U.S. government bonds issued at a discount, redeemed at full face value at maturity. They are called *accrual* securities, meaning that interest is credited, or accrued, periodically, increasing the bond's total redemption value. Interest is paid only when a bond is redeemed.
Minimum deposit	$25
Holding period	Generally 10 years, although Congress can extend that date. If you redeem a savings bond early, you'll receive lower interest (see *Return*, below).
Tax status	Exempt from state and local taxes; federal taxes deferred until redeemed.
Return	Here's an example: You buy a $50 bond for $25. The bond has been issued with a six percent minimum rate, which means it will reach maturity in 12 years. If you keep if for the full 12 years, you'll get $50 back.
How to buy	From commercial banks or in person at Federal Reserve banks. From the Bureau of Public Debt, Parkersburg, WV, 26106-1328. Full details of exchange offerings may be found in the Department of the Treasury Circular, Public Debt Series #2-80. All U.S. Savings Bonds may be registered in the name of a single owner, or co-owners, or beneficiaries. Social Security numbers of the owners are required to be inscribed on the back.

(continued on next page)

VEHICLE	SERIES EE SAVINGS BONDS
What's good about them	Safety Low minimum deposit makes them easy to buy.
What to watch for	Reset interest rates on occasion. People tend to forget about them and hold them past maturity, resulting in a stepped down level of interest.

Table 15: Series HH Savings Bonds

VEHICLE	SERIES HH SAVINGS BONDS
Brief definition	U.S. government bonds which are issued as *current-income* securities, meaning that they pay interest semi-annually, either by check or electronic funds transfer.
Minimum deposit	$500
Holding period	10 years.
Tax status	Exempt from state and local taxes; federal taxes deferred until redeemed.
Return	Semi-annual interest payments are as follows: *Denomination* *Payment* $500 $15 1,000 30 5,000 150 10,000 300
How to buy	Same as Series EE
What's good about it	Safety

Table 16: Mortgage-Backed Securities

VEHICLE	MORTGAGE-BACKED SECURITIES *(Ginnie Mae, Fannie Mae, Freddie Mac)*
Brief definition	Securities issued by various agencies, and backed by mortgages. They are basically a pool of mortgage loans. When a bank issues a mortgage, it typically puts that mortgage in a pool or bundle with other mortgages. The bank that holds the mortgage, that issued the security, collects the monthly loan payments from the homeowner and passes them on to the buyer of the security. These securities are always backed by an agency which guarantees payment to the ultimate investor.
Variations	*Ginnie Maes*, the most popular mortgaged-backed securities, are issued by the Government National Mortgage Association (GNMA), an agency of the U.S. Department of Housing and Urban Development. *Fannie Maes* are issued by the Federal National Mortgage Association (FNMA), a publicly owned, government-sponsored corporation. *Freddie Macs* are issued by the Federal Home Mortgage Corporation (FLHMC), a publicly chartered agency. *Collateralized mortgage obligations (CMOs)* are a variety of mortgaged-backed securities, pooled together and separated into different time frames for repayment (if you wanted a fast return, you'd buy 5-year CMOs; for a long-term investment you'd go for 20-year CMOs).

(continued on next page)

Vehicle	Mortgage-Backed Securities *(Ginnie Mae, Fannie Mae, Freddie Mac)*
Minimum deposit	Certificates representing a bundle are issued in denominations of at least $1,000,000. These certificates are sold to a broker who will, in turn, slice them up and sell shares of the whole (in minimum denominations of $25,000) to individual investors, mutual funds or unit trusts.
Holding period	1 to 40 years
Tax status	All taxable
How to buy	Through a broker or fund
What's good about them	Interest rates are higher than treasury bonds; the risk is slightly higher, but still well within the general range I'd describe as safe.
What to watch for	You never can be certain how much money you'll receive each month and how long installments will last. That's because homeowners often pay off the mortgages ahead of time. Prepayments are so common that Ginnie Maes backed by 30-year mortgages actually have an average life of 10 to 20 years. CMOs give you a better idea of when your principal will be returned, but a lot of people consider them too complicated and risky for the average investor. The risk comes from the fact that you never know exactly what's in a CMO until after the fact.

Table 17: High-Grade Corporate Bonds

VEHICLE	HIGH GRADE CORPORATE BONDS
Brief definition	Debt instruments issued by a private corporation as opposed to any form of government security.
Variations	*Debentures:* These are also known as unsecured bonds. They are general obligations of the company, and not backed up by particular assets. *Equipment Trust Certificates:* These are usually issued by railroads. They are certificates of ownership interest in specific equipment, for instance, specific locomotives. The trustee for the equipment trust leases the equipment to the railroad at a rental price. These are bonds because they are debt instruments, but ownership interests in that if the company can't repay, you could theoretically find yourself with a locomotive in your backyard. They're not a good idea for the average investor. *Guaranteed bonds:* These are backed by another corporation. *Income bonds:* If you hold one of these, you may already have experienced a run of bad luck, since they're usually issued to holders of defaulted bonds after a reorganization. Interest payments are contingent upon the company's earnings. *Convertible bonds or debentures:* These may be exchanged by the holder for a specified number of shares of common stock. Generally, they'd pay slightly less than other comparable bonds, but hold out the possibility of capital growth if you decide to convert them to stock. They can provide a great deal of flexibility.
Minimum deposit	$1000

VEHICLE	HIGH GRADE CORPORATE BONDS
Holding period	1 to 30 years
Tax status	Taxable
How to buy	Through a broker. Brokers can charge varying markups on these transactions, so it's a good idea to stick with bonds listed in the financial newspapers, so you know, when you buy or sell, what kind of markup your broker is going to charge.
What's good about them	Higher rate of return than Treasuries or municipal bonds.
What to watch for	Bonds issued by corporations are typically riskier than Treasuries. If you're buying corporate bonds, make sure you stick with the high grade ones — there's less chance of the issuer getting in trouble. There's also less chance of issuers getting in trouble if you give them less time to get in trouble. With corporate bonds, you're better off staying with shorter term maturities —say, an average life of 5 years. The longer the maturity, the greater the risk. This is less true if you're buying bonds from extremely well-established companies with AAA ratings. Laddering and diversification are particularly good ideas if you're going to invest in corporate bonds. Here are a couple of other risks you're taking on with corporate bonds: *Event risk:* A company may be taken over in a buyout, and the new buyer may issue new debt.

(continued on next page)

VEHICLE	HIGH GRADE CORPORATE BONDS
What to watch for	*Call risk:* Most issuers specify that they have the right to redeem the bond before maturity—usually 5–10 years after the bonds are issued. If your bond is called, the issuer may pay you a premium. However, it could be worth a year's interest. *Yield risk:* This is when greed takes over. You're lured by high yields (see junk bonds), and you overlook the total return. If you fall into this one, you may be getting a great yield while your initial investment is shrinking because the issuer's financial situation has been growing worse and worse. Here's a good rule of thumb: An unusually high yield generally means someone is trolling for fish to bite.

Table 18: Certificates of Deposit

VEHICLE	CERTIFICATES OF DEPOSIT (CDs)
Brief definition	A debt instrument issued by a bank.
Minimum deposit	$100
Holding period	From a few weeks to several years
Tax status	Taxable
How to buy	From a bank
What's good about it	If under $100,000 per depositor, guaranteed by FDIC.
What to watch for	Low returns. In fact, after taxes, returns may not keep up with inflation.

JUNK BONDS

Stay away from these. They were glamour investments in the 1980s, and they remain as a symbol of the excesses of those years—Michael Milken and Drexel Burnham Lambert are vivid symbols of the destructiveness of junk bond fever out of control. Drexel Burnham Lambert specialized in leveraged buyouts of companies. These buyouts were paid for by the issuance of risky but high-yielding bonds—a house of cards that came crashing down when many of the bonds defaulted in the late 1980s and early 1990s.

Junk bonds either have no rating, or are rated low by the official bond rating services.

Mutual Funds

Table 19: Mutual Funds

VEHICLE	MUTUAL FUNDS
Brief definition	A professionally managed company that raises money from shareholders and invests it in a variety of ways, depending on the type of risk-return potential desired.
Variations	Listed below
Minimum deposit	$50–$2000
Tax status	Depends on the fund
How to buy	Through a mutual fund company or a broker
What's good about it	Diversification and professional management

(continued on next page)

VEHICLE	MUTUAL FUNDS
What to watch for	Track record: See how well the fund has done in the past 3 to 5 years. This, of course, is no guarantee that it will continue to do well, especially if the record was created by a fund manager who has left.
Fees:	All funds are going to charge some kind of management fee, typically 1% of the amount invested. All funds are going to have to describe their fees in their prospectus, and even provide you with a table showing you how their expenses and fees will affect a hypothetical $1,000 investment. There are five major categories of fees: Not all funds charge all of these fees. Make sure you know which ones are being charged by any fund you're interested in. *Loads* are a sales commission paid up front when you invest in a fund. I recommend avoiding load funds. A high load can drag down the performance of a fund. *Management and expense fees* are charged annually for managing the fund. They typically range from .25% to 1.5% of the amount invested. *12b-1* fees are named after Rule 12b-1 in the Investment Company Act of 1940, which permitted mutual funds to charge fees to cover marketing and advertising costs. They typically range from .25% to 1.5% of the amount invested. *Exit or redemption fees* are charged when you sell your shares. They range from a flat $5 to 2% of the amount withdrawn.

(continued on next page)

VEHICLE	MUTUAL FUNDS
Fees:	*Back-end load,* also charged when you take money out of a fund, is designed to discourage frequent trading in the fund, especially in the early years. It can be as high as 6% at first, but then usually it scales back each year, until by the time you've held the fund for 6 years, it disappears. Try to stay away from these unless you're in for the long haul and it doesn't matter. Don't invest in a fund just before a distribution of interest, dividends, or capital gains. You'll only be getting back the money you've just put in, and paying taxes on it.

Here's a rundown on the major varieties of mutual funds:

Table 20: Fixed Income Funds

VEHICLE	FIXED INCOME FUNDS
Brief definition	A fund that invests in bonds that pay a fixed rate of return.
What's good about it	It can help smooth out a portfolio's volatility, and it can perform well, especially during a time of declining interest rates.
What to watch for	Invest gradually when you place money in a bond fund—otherwise, you can lose money if interest rates suddenly move up. Avoid funds that charge commissions when you reinvest your distributions. Don't focus on yield and forget total return. Look for a large fixed-income fund. It will have the clout to obtain the best securities.

Table 21: Stock Funds

VEHICLE	STOCK FUNDS
Brief definition	Mutual funds that invest in stocks.
Variations	Stock funds may be either conservative *income funds,* specializing in stable stocks that will reliably pay higher dividends, or *growth funds,* specializing in stocks which are expected to increase in value, but may pay little to no dividends.
What's good about it	In the long run, stocks have historically been the best performers of any investment vehicle.
What to watch for	In the short run, stocks can be volatile. Make sure you have the right kind of stock fund for your needs. Growth stocks tend to outperform income stocks in the long run, but are much more likely to drop sharply during falling markets.

Table 22: Balanced Funds

VEHICLE	BALANCED FUNDS
Brief definition	A mixture of stocks and bonds.
What's good about it	Diversification—stocks and bonds don't always rise and fall in value at the same rate.
What to watch for	Make sure you know what kind of mixture you're getting. Read the prospectus—each balanced fund will list its ratio of types of investments.

Table 23: Growth and Income Funds

Vehicle	Growth and Income Funds
Brief definition	A stock fund that contains both growth and income stocks.
What's good about it	Safer than growth alone, more of a potential for growth than income alone.
What to watch for	The reverse of the coin—less growth than growth funds, more volatility than income funds.

Table 24: Unit Investment Trusts

Vehicle	Unit Investment Trusts
Brief definition	An investment vehicle in which the securities are not managed—there's no buying or selling during the life of the fund. Instead, there's one round of purchasing of various securities, typically bonds. Then after a period of time, everything is sold and the investors get their money back.
Holding period	1 to 30 years
What's good about it	Not much overhead—you're not paying the high management fees you'd pay with other mutual funds.

Table 25: Capital Appreciation Funds

VEHICLE	CAPITAL APPRECIATION FUNDS
Brief definition	This is an aggressive growth fund that aims for high returns by speculative investments, such as stock in small companies with a potential for large growth, or volatile securities. They may also take risks by trading with borrowed money or *short selling,* a kind of speculation that relies on a drop in the market.
What's good about it	Potential for high profits.
What to watch for	You could lose your shirt, unless you're investing extra money you can afford to speculate with.

Table 26: International Funds

VEHICLE	INTERNATIONAL FUNDS
Brief definition	A fund that invests on foreign stock exchanges, including the Tokyo, Paris, and London exchanges. International funds can also invest in foreign bonds.
What's good about it	Many financial advisors believe that it can provide an extra degree of diversification.
What to watch for	Coups, devaluation, earthquakes, trade wars.

Table 27: Index Funds

VEHICLE	INDEX FUNDS
Brief definition	A fund that creates a portfolio from the stocks that make up the leading market indexes, such as the Standard and Poor's 500.
What's good about it	The fund is supposed to mirror the index, so you shouldn't do any worse than average.
What to watch for	Specific weightings may exaggerate fund performance.

Table 28: Money Market Funds

VEHICLE	MONEY MARKET FUNDS
Brief definition	A highly liquid fund that invests in short-term debt instruments.
Variations	*Taxable money market funds* invest in instruments such as treasury bills, government agency notes, CDs, commercial paper, and overnight loans to banks and brokers called repurchase agreements. *Tax-exempt money market funds* invest in short-term municipal bonds.
Minimum deposit	$500 to $2000
Tax status	Taxable funds are taxable, tax exempt funds are tax exempt.
How to buy	Open an account by buying shares in a fund.
What's good about it	Liquidity. Interest—usually higher than bank rates, and credited to your account frequently, even every day.

Here are a few excellent sources for information on mutual funds:

Mutual Fund Education Alliance
1900 Erie St., Suite 120
Kansas City, MO 64116

100 Percent No-Load Council
1501 Broadway, Suite 312
New York, NY 10036

The Investment Company Institute, a trade group, publishes a guide listing 3,000 funds and their phone numbers, and the minimum investment they'll take. For the guide, send $5 to:

The Directory of Mutual Funds
Investment Company Institute
P.O. Box 66140
Washington, D.C. 20035–614

Cash Equivalents

These are bank or non-bank instruments that can easily be converted to cash, without your having to wait or sell something. They're all low-risk instruments, and most reguire little, if any, minimum deposit.

Table 29: Savings Accounts

VEHICLE	SAVINGS ACCOUNTS
Brief definition	Money that's deposited in your account at a bank.
What's good about it	Extremely safe; insured by the Federal Deposit Insurance Corporation (as long as your accounts are below FDIC limits).
What to watch for	Extremely low return. Interest on funds in a savings account may not even keep pace with investment. You'd use a savings account primarily as a place to build cash to invest, and a place to park cash that you'll need quickly for large expenses, such as emergencies, funding your monthly checking account needs, paying large bills (such as college tuition), etc.

Table 30: Now Accounts

VEHICLE	NOW ACCOUNTS
Brief definition	A savings-type account at a bank which generally has some kind of minimum deposit and minimum balance, and allows you to write only a limited number of checks per month, usually three. Interest is generally lower than a savings account.
What you'd use it for	To fund your other accounts

Table 31: One-Year Certificates of Deposit

VEHICLE	ONE-YEAR CERTIFICATES OF DEPOSIT
Brief definition	See above. There is a penalty for early withdrawal, but you can get your money from them quickly, so they are considered to be liquid.

Table 32: Treasury Bills

VEHICLE	TREASURY BILLS
Brief definition	See above. These are not formally liquid in that the treasury won't buy them back, but you can get your money from them quickly, so they are considered to be liquid.

10

Making Provisions

At some point—at least one point—during your tenure as parent, your child is going to turn to you and shout, "I didn't ask to be born!"

There are a number of first-class rejoinders to this, including, "Neither did anyone else," "Maybe not, but you still have to clean the garage," and the ever-popular "Don't talk to me in that tone of voice, young lady!"

Your children didn't ask to be born, but they owe you certain things nonetheless, like cleaning out the garage and not talking to you in that tone of voice.

You, on the other hand, did ask for them to be born, and that means you have some very real obligations to them. You've agreed to a living contract, and that is to provide for them, or to make sure they are provided for, until they're capable of providing for themselves.

That's all. You haven't obligated yourself, like the heroine of some nineteenth-century romantic novel, to stand on a Times Square corner selling apples so that your daughter can go to debutante balls. But you have undertaken a very solemn obligation to give your kids a fair shake—even if you're not around to do it yourself.

That means you have to do a thorough job of thinking the unthinkable, and preparing for it. That means putting your affairs in order. That means insurance, wills, and trusts.

Life Insurance

In this section, I'm going to offer you a formula that you can use in determining how much life insurance you should think about buying. But keep in mind that this is just a guideline to help your thought process, not a set of rules for actual purchasing. You must personalize your own situation—there is no one universal formula to fit all people.

Also, as you enter into this process, remember the purpose of life insurance. What life insurance is for, and all that it should be for, is: to temporarily replace income, to take care of large obligations, and pay debts. It is not a measure of your personal worth, a legacy to your loved ones, or a yardstick to measure how much you love them. It's not supposed to be a windfall, but a guarantee that your standard of living will be maintained.

To figure out how much you'll need in an insurance package, the basic formula is as simple—or as complicated—as estimating your future expenses.

Here's one tip as you start to make that estimate: Most people tend to underestimate the amount of life insurance they need and overestimate the amount of property insurance.

Even more likely to be underestimated—and potentially even more serious if you do underestimate it—is disability insurance.

Because you need disability insurance for the same reason you need life insurance—to replace income, to get your family through a period where you can't provide for them—I'm including it in this chapter.

Americans between the ages of 35 and 65 are much more likely to become disabled than to die. According to Don Underwood and Paul B. Brown in *Grow Rich Slowly* (Viking,

1993), one-third of all people will be disabled for three months or longer between the ages of 30 and 65.

Even if you have disability insurance as part of the medical coverage provided by your employer, don't count on it being enough. Employer-provided disability coverage is likely to be lean, and usually is short-term. Check to find out what you have; and if it's not adequate, consider supplementing it.

If the purpose of insurance is primarily to make sure your standard of living is maintained for your dependents, then it follows logically—although all too often, people tend to forget this—that as your dependents grow up, their dependency will decrease. In other words, you need more insurance when your kids are young—and your financial assets are leaner. When they get older, when they finish school and become self-supporting, and your own nest egg has grown more substantial . . . well, frankly, you don't need as much. You may want to keep a life insurance policy as a pension for your spouse, but you should remember to keep reevaluating your insurance needs as your life circumstances change.

Constructing the Formula

The first step in estimating your needs is to calculate your current situation. You'll do this in four steps:

First, figure the *immediate expenses* that your family would incur if you or your spouse suddenly died (and to do a complete job on both this and the next step, you really have to figure the consequences of both of you suddenly dying). Immediate expenses are the ones that will be incurred at your death and, generally speaking, because of your death.

Second, figure the *future expenses* your family can expect to incur. Future expenses represent a much more substantial amount. They'll include money for family living expenses, emergencies, child care, education—all the day-to-day and long-term expenses that you plan to cover with your paycheck and your investments.

Third, calculate all the assets you currently have that can go toward covering all those expenses.

Finally, subtract the assets from the expenses. The difference will be the amount that you need to cover with insurance.

Immediate Expenses

EXPENSE	PARTNER 1	PARTNER 2	AMOUNT
Funeral			
Probate expenses			
Federal estate taxes			
State inheritance taxes			
Uninsured medical costs			
Outstanding debts			
Total immediate expenses			

IMMEDIATE EXPENSES

Here's a detailed breakdown of immediate expenses, with some guidelines on how to estimate them.

Funeral costs: There's a tremendous range here, depending on how elaborate you want to get. The National Funeral Directors Association says that the national average (as of 1995) is $4,000, but this does not include cemetery expenses, monuments, clergy fees, and transportation. Even if you're figuring on a relatively simple funeral, I'd suggest putting this figure at $5,000 to be on the safe side—and, of course, it can be a great deal higher.

Probate costs: Probate is the legal process by which the state validates your will after you die and makes sure that your debts are paid and your wishes are carried out. Your will may have to go through probate, especially if you have property in your own name, give property to your children, or set up trusts. This probate procedure will probably include lawyers, plus fees for filing, plus fees to your executor.

Attorney's fees will vary, depending on the lawyer and the state. Some states set a maximum charge based on a percentage of the estate's value. Others require "reasonable fees" based on actual work. Even if you die without a will (which I certainly hope and trust none of my readers will do!), there will still be costs. The state will distribute your property and charge your estate for its work.

For purposes of this worksheet, figure that you'll need 2 percent to 5 percent of the total estate to cover federal estate taxes, state inheritance taxes, and probate costs.

Estate taxes: Federal estate taxes come into effect when the estate is valued in excess of $600,000. State taxes vary in different states; some states allow a person to pass her/his entire estate to a spouse tax-free. Check with a tax specialist to see what applies to you—and remember if you move to a different state, you may need to recheck this.

Uninsured medical costs: A lingering and ultimately fatal illness can be financially devastating if it's not completely covered by health insurance. If you're not covered for this contingency, you'd better budget several thousand dollars here to be on the safe side—or better yet, take the money and buy health insurance.

Future Expenses

FUTURE EXPENSES	EXPENSE	NO. OF YEARS	TOTAL
Monthly household expenses (x 12)			
Mortgage/rent (monthly payment x 12)			
Mortgage (lump sum payment)			
Child care expenses			
School expenses (child's name)			
College expenses (child's name)			

(continued on next page)

FUTURE EXPENSES	EXPENSE	NO. OF YEARS	TOTAL
Long-term repayment of debt			
Emergency money			
Total future expenses			
Total expenses			

FUTURE EXPENSES

Monthly household expenses: For this item, start with your monthly expenses (leaving out the large expenses enumerated below) that you figured for your first Consolidation worksheet in Chapter 2. Calculate 75 percent of that figure. At the point where you start needing this table, one of you will be gone. It costs one person less to live than it does two people, but more than half as much.

Mortgage: Decide whether you want your survivors to have the money to go on making monthly payments, or whether you want your insurance proceeds to pay off the mortgage totally. Enter whichever of these figures is appropriate. Of course, if you are paying rent, you'll be using the monthly figure.

Child care expenses: This may just be part of your regular monthly household expenses. It could be an added expense, though, if one of you is currently staying home with the kids, and if you assume that will no longer be possible. Child care expenses can fall within a broad spectrum—anywhere from $4,000 to $15,000 a year, depending on the kind of child care you'll need. Don't forget that as your children get older, their needs can move from full-time child care, to part-time child care, to no child care.

School and college expenses: Enter these separately for each child. Use the figures you've calculated previously in the education chapter, Chapter 6.

Repayment of debt: Your largest debt, of course, is your mortgage, and this is a separate category. Here, list car loans, bank loans, credit card payments that you're making on time, etc.

Emergency money: It's a good idea to figure in $10,000–$15,000 here, or three months of after tax income. There's no absolute standard—this is a variable expense in making your insurance plans.

Assets

ASSET	AMOUNT
Cash/Savings	
Equity in real estate	
Stocks/bonds/mutual funds	
IRA/Keogh-type plans	
Employer savings plans	
Lump-sum employee pension	
Current life insurance	

(continued on next page)

Asset	Amount
Social Security survivors' benefits	
Other assets	
Total assets	

ASSETS

Lump-sum employee pension: If you are covered by a pension plan at work, check with your pension administrators to see if there will be a lump sum survivor's benefit payable upon your death. If there is, include it among your assets.

Current life insurance: If you already have any life insurance policies, including employer-purchased group insurance plans that cover life, include the benefits you'd get from them among your assets.

Social Security survivors' benefits: For many families, Social Security survivors' benefits are a major source of income when the primary breadwinner dies, and they should be considered as part of a family's income and assets when estimating life insurance needs.

The monthly payments your survivors receive is based on a percentage of a certain "magic number" that the Social

Security Administration (SSA) calculates for you, based on your earnings record. Several factors determine this payment:

A surviving spouse who is under age 60 receives benefits only if he/she is taking care of small children and does not have substantial earnings. These benefits stop when the youngest child turns 16.

If the spouse is caring for a child who was disabled before age 22, he/she will receive benefits for as long as the child remains disabled.

SSA will also pay benefits to surviving children until they are 18, regardless of whether their mother or father receives a benefit.

SSA will compute your benefit for you if you fill out and return their form SSA–7004. You can request the form by calling (800) 937-2000.

Constructing the Formula—Totals

Total expenses	
Total assets	
Additional insurance needed (expenses minus assets)	

Varieties of Life Insurance

Table 33: Term Insurance

Why you'd want it	Term insurance is generally speaking, the cheapest kind of policy you can buy—and that is, in fact, the main reason you'd want it. It's primarily for young people who really can't afford anything else, and who have major expenses in their lives, like a mortgage or kids' college fund, that their survivors simply would not be able to handle.

(continued on next page)

Why you'd want it	It's also the simplest. What it does is exactly what you'd expect—no more, no less. It insures that there'll be something to replace your life. You pay premiums, and in exchange, the policy pays a sum of money to your beneficiaries if you die. The price will vary with the amount of coverage that you want, with your age and health.
What you should watch for	You don't want to keep this policy forever—in fact, that's why it's called term insurance. Basically, premiums are computed on the basis of the odds of your living through that particular year, so your premium will probably increase over time, and may rise so much that the costs are out of sight. Renewing yearly gives you the cheapest basic rate, or you can pay a little more for a *premium guarantee*—a guarantee that they won't raise your rate for a period of five or ten years. A new physical exam may be required periodically, In some policies, you can trade off a yearly physical exam for an automatic rate increase. If you have an option to renew, there is often an age at which the policy ceases, usually 65 or 70. If you're keeping your term insurance this long (in general, not a good idea) make sure you buy a guaranteed renewable policy.
What you'd use it for	This is the best kind to buy if you need insurance for a limited period of time, in a fixed amount. If you have young children, or you're planning a family, you know that you're going to need to save a lot of money for their college education. If something happens to you, you'll want to make sure that's taken care of.

(continued on next page)

| What you'd use it for | The same goes for your mortgage. For example, with children, I recommend buying term insurance on your life to protect them until they are through college. After that, they are (theoretically) on their own, and the big expense of college is no longer something that has to be covered. Term insurance is also good to cover mortgage payments or other major debt after the death of one spouse. You might consider, for example, buying a term policy to run the length of your mortgage. |

Table 34: Whole Life (or Straight Life) Insurance

Why you'd want it	This is the most widely sold type of insurance in the U.S. It's the most flexible, and its premiums remain the same for the entire lifetime of the insured. The amount of the premium is determined by your age and does not increase as long as the policy is in force. Therefore, the younger you are when you buy a whole life policy, the cheaper the premiums.
What you should watch for	*Cost.* This is the main reason a young family might want to use term insurance, either as a supplement to, or temporary substitute for, whole life. Keep in mind that it's tremendously important to shop around for a life insurance policy, since there are no regulations on the cost of insurance policies. For that matter, the true cost of a policy is not always that easy to assess. The premiums are only part of the story, since most whole life policies pay a dividend that is a return of premium. If you figure that in, then the higher the dividend, the lower the real cost of the premium. *Misplaced resources.* Don't plan to use a whole life policy as a savings vehicle—there are other ways to save more quickly and with a better return.

(continued on next page)

What you'd use it for	*Payment on death.* This, of course, is the basic use for any life insurance policy.
	Savings. During the first few years that you pay into a whole life policy, the insurance company will credit a small amount of your premiums to a "savings account" that will build up as time goes on. This savings account is yours, like any other savings account, even if you cancel the policy, and you can borrow against it from the insurance company, at a rate of interest that's stated on your policy.
	In fairness, though I don't recommend using an insurance policy as a savings vehicle, insurance professionals will point out that a policy's cash value builds up tax deferred, which could be attractive to people in the higher tax brackets.
	If you do borrow against the policy, you'll still continue to pay your premium at the same rate you always have. But if you die, the insurance company will deduct the amount you've borrowed from the amount it pays your beneficiary.
	This "policy loan" provision can be an extra source of capital when you need a large sum of money — for college or any sort of emergency.
	Dividends. You can structure a whole life policy to pay you dividends, which are not taxable since they are considered a return of excess premiums you have paid, and not real "unearned income," which is what dividends from stocks are considered.
Combining the two	You can also put a *Term insurance rider* on a whole life policy, which should be convertible to whole life. You cannot borrow against the term insurance rider.

Table 35: Universal Life Insurance

Why you'd want it	*Cost.* It's cheaper than whole life, though more expensive than term insurance. *Flexibility.* This is a hybrid of a whole life insurance policy with a tax-deferred investment program. It also offers adjustable features that allow you, as the policy holder, to change the face amount (death benefit) or the premium level to suit your changing needs over the years. Some years you might put in more money towards the policy, thus building up its cash value faster; in other, leaner years, you'd be putting in less. *Borrowing.* You can borrow against it at favorable rates, without increasing your tax liability.
What you should watch for	Although universal life generally pays a more competitive interest rate than a whole life policy, you have to make sure you know how this works on your particular policy. Universal life rates are adjustable, and fluctuate with current rates. which means that it's possible for a company to offer a high initial rate to entice buyers, then lower it later. The mortality rates and expense charges may rise within the contract period. If this happens, your costs are increased, and the amount available for investment is decreased. Each year, you must decide how much you want to invest in the policy, which means you can't just buy it and forget. It's another thing you have to keep track of. The IRS imposes a maximum funding level on universal life policies, which means that you can't increase the investment portion of your policy without increasing life insurance coverage . . . and for the most part, as you get older, you may well find that there's no reason why you'd want to do this.

(continued on next page)

What you'd use it for	You might want it if you planned to use insurance as part of an investment program, and you like a hands-on approach.

Table 36: Variable Life Insurance

Why you'd want it	*Flexibility:* Combining permanent insurance protection with a flexible investment plan, variable life lets you invest the cash value in a broad range of investments. *Diversity:* You can select your own portfolio mix among a wide range of choices: stocks, bonds, money market instruments, etc. *Cost:* Like universal life, this falls between whole life and term insurance.
What you should watch for	*Risk:* With whole life, a minimum death benefit is guaranteed. Here, your death benefits may increase if your investments do well, or they could fall in value if they do poorly. *Inflexibility:* Once you've bought the policy, you can't change the amount you pay. *Uncertain future:* Although variable life is technically a life insurance product, it falls into the category of a tax-advantaged investment. That means Congress can modify or eliminate the advantage of a tax-free investment at any time.
What you'd use it for	Again, this would be a personal choice for those who want more control.

(continued on next page)

Table 37: Single Premium Life Insurance

Why you'd want it	*Settled once and for all:* This is a whole life policy that you pay for in one lump sum up front. There is a cash portion. They usually have a minimum requirement of $5,000. *Tax advantages:* The cash buildup is tax deferred. *Borrowing:* You can borrow against it at any time.
What you should watch for	*Back-end load:* This means that you'll be charged if you make withdrawals during a certain time. Many companies impose this. Check and see what the terms of your policy are.
What you'd use it for	In case of a windfall

Table 38: Disability Insurance

Why you'd want it	Because you can't do without it. Any illness or accident that keeps you out of work for an extended period of time can eat up your savings as surely as your death will.
What you should watch for	*Duplication:* If you have some disability insurance through your job, or workmen's compensation, buy enough insurance that, when added to what you already have, will allow you to maintain your standard of living. It's worth noting that the higher your income, the less likely your employer's benefit package is to be adequate for maintaining your lifestyle.

(continued on next page)

Why you'd want it	*Fine print:* Some policies say that if you do some kind of work when you're disabled, they will pay no benefits or reduced benefits. The best policies pay benefits if your disability renders you incapable of performing your own occupation.
	Cost: Basically, three things affect the cost and quality of disability coverage: First, the length of the waiting period until the policy begins paying benefits: the longer the waiting period, the cheaper the policy. Second, the length of time the policy will continue to pay benefits. What you want to look for is a policy that will pay until age 65, when you start to collect Social Security. Third, how the policy defines disability You want one that will pay if you're unable to work at your own job or profession.
What you'd use it for	People are living longer these days, and it's becoming more likely, as a result, that some part of your life will be spent in a nursing home or under some form of medical care and supervision. Underwood and Brown, in *Grow Rich Slowly*, say that Americans 65 or older face a 40% chance of spending some time in a nursing home.
	Long-term care protection: This is a specialized but important form of disability protection. Many of us are starting our families later these days. One thing that means is that we may need extended care at a point when our children are just starting their own families, and least equipped to help us either financially or in terms of time.

And Keep in Mind . . .

There are no fixed prices for insurance. Shop around. There are no federal regulations for insurance companies—

it's all state by state. Make sure you know your own state's regulations.

The price of a policy is important, but it can't be the only consideration. The stability of the insurance company is just as important. Find a company that's financially sound. A. M. Best is a financial rating service that rates insurance companies. By the way, Best's ratings aren't infallible; the service can be caught unawares if an insurance company suddenly declares insolvency. And another point in relation to Best's—you'll want to check any insurance company's ratings if you're considering buying stock.

Avoid smooth-talking agents who are trying to sell, rather than help. Make sure that you see every promise they've made in writing.

Wills

The first, and most important, thing about wills is: You have to have one. And if you're like most people, you don't.

I'm not just exaggerating for effect. About two-thirds of all Americans die without ever making out a will.

It's an easy thing to put off. No one likes to think about dying, and it's easy to think that, well, there'll be time to deal with that later, when I'm older.

But the critical time to be absolutely sure you are covered by the protection of a will is when your kids are younger, when they're really vulnerable, and when dying intestate (without a will) could be more than aggravation . . . it could be devastating.

How devastating? All right, let's look at it, starting with the worst possible scenario—which doesn't have to do with money, but with guardianship. If you and your spouse both die—or if you die as a single parent—and you haven't left a will, your children become the responsibility of the probate court. A probate judge will decide who they'll live with—their future will be in the hands of a stranger. The judge will normally pick a relative, but not necessarily the relative you would have chosen; you might not have chosen a relative at all. Your children could end up not only with someone you might not approve of, but even conceivably with someone who might not like or want them.

So a crucial part of your will has to be provision for the guardianship of your children. Here are some things you should think about in planning a guardianship in your will:

First, make sure that the prospective guardian wants the responsibility. Actually, the very first thing is to make sure the prospective guardian *knows* about the responsibility. Yes, there have been cases of an astonished relative or friend finding out for the first time, when the will is read, that he is suddenly the new daddy of three small children.

Talk to the person, or the couple, that you want to have taking care of your kids. Make sure of the following:

Would they accept the children wholeheartedly, or are they just "willing to take them"? If it's the latter, you might want to do some serious rethinking. It's possible that they're being guarded because they don't want to sound too enthusiastic about the prospect of your death. But it also could be that, much as they may love you and your kids, they really aren't ready to take on that kind of responsibility.

If you—and they—are satisfied that they really are the right couple, then you have to sit down together and figure out the answers to some other nitty-gritty questions. When you've worked through the next worksheet, it's time for a visit to your insurance agent, as well as your lawyer or whoever is making out your will.

My general philosophy of insurance, as I've explained before, is that its purpose is to make up financially for your absence, not to provide a giant financial windfall for someone. You don't want to make yourself insurance-poor, so that you end up wondering if you're better off dead.

As I explain this worksheet—and as you make it out—you may end up feeling that you're nickel-and-diming your beloved sister and brother-in-law or your best friends; they may end up feeling they're gouging you for too much.

Try not to get too emotional about it. Remember, you're just making a contingency plan for something that probably won't happen. The best alternative, if any of you start worrying if these figures are really fair, is just to shrug and say, "Well, Neale says they're OK." Seriously—this is touchy stuff, and you do want to keep it as light, matter-of-fact, and unemotional as possible.

For "Expenses per length of guardianship," fill in a figure that represents what that expense would be if you were to die tomorrow. You'll have to use different formulas to come up with those figures.

Building a new wing on a house, or moving to a larger house, is a one-time expense. The figures in the second and third column are going to be the same.

Note, however, that if the prospective guardian is a renter, this will be a different story. If a family has to rent a larger house or apartment, then figure that expense at the probable difference in rent between the old place and the new place, extended over the number of years until your *youngest* child reaches eighteen.

Expenses for Guardianship

	EXPENSES PER YEAR	EXPENSES PER LENGTH OF GUARDIANSHIP
New house/apartment		
Remodeling existing structure		
Food		
Clothing		
Child care		

(continued on next page)

	EXPENSES PER YEAR	EXPENSES PER LENGTH OF GUARDIANSHIP
Private school		
School supplies		
College		
Summer camp		
Family vacations		
Enrichment expenses		
Miscellaneous		
TOTAL		

For these and all subsequent figures, you'll have to make some sort of a guess at inflation. I suggest using a formula modeled on the Fidelity College Savings Plan's table. That uses a 6 percent inflation estimate, which is about right for college costs but a little high for normal inflation, but that's OK. It builds in a little margin for unexpected expenses.

In this case, since you're planning on continual expenses over a number of years, rather than try to estimate an expense for a given year in the future, use the table that follows to derive a median. I'll explain that below.

Table 39: Inflation Factors for Guardianships

Years of Guardianship	Inflation Factor	Years of Guardianship	Inflation Factor
1	1.06	10	1.79
2	1.12	11	1.90
3	1.19	12	2.01
4	1.26	13	2.13
5	1.24	14	2.26
6	1.42	15	2.40
7	1.50	16	2.54
8	1.59	17	2.69
9	1.69	18	2.85

Let's say your youngest child is four years old, which would mean 14 years of guardianship, and let's say your prospective guardian would need to rent a house that would be an extra $1000 a month.

That works out like this:

Expenses per year	$1,000
× 7-year inflation figure (median for 14 years)	1.50
Subtotal	$1,500
× years of guardianship	14
Expenses per length of guardianship:	$21,000

For expenses like food and clothing, you'll have to figure for each child separately.

For your child's education expenses, you should already have those figured, so it's just a question of plugging them in.

One note of caution here. Things in life don't always work out the way we planned them. You know you'll have to be flexible during your own life; if your life is cut short, you have to realize—and this can be harder—that those you've left behind will have to be flexible, too. For example, if you've set up a master plan for your kids to go to Yale, and you're talking to prospective guardians who plan to send their kids to a state college, then you're asking them to create a situation in their own homes, somewhere down the line, that simply is not going to be fair. And you can't ask it.

Once you've completed this worksheet, and you have a figure that you can use, take out a term insurance policy, naming the prospective guardians as beneficiaries, and creating a custodial account for the purpose of meeting your children's expenses.

Make sure that there's a specific provision for the actual transfer of money to the guardian's account. My sister Alison is the designated guardian for Kyle and Rhett, and we did sit down together and make out a worksheet. I've taken out a term insurance policy, and specified that in the event of my death, a sum of money adequate for covering the kids' needs will be automatically deposited in her account every month.

It's worth noting that the designated guardian of your child doesn't also have to be the person that handles the assets you've left for the support of your children. Sometimes the most loving and nurturing person isn't also the best at handling money. Sometimes the handling of money can be complicated. If you have a substantial estate, or your assets are of a kind that need careful management, you can designate another person—for instance, a lawyer, banker, financial planner, or CPA—to do the actual asset managing, in cooperation with the guardian. A hint: If you're doing it this way, try to make sure that you're choosing two parties who get along with each other.

Don't forget what you've done here. Like all your other financial worksheets, a will is not something to be stuck into a drawer of safe deposit box and never looked at again. If the circumstances of your prospective guardian change, you may want to reconsider. Changed circumstances can include:

Divorce: As a single parent, your prospective guardian may simply not be able to handle an expanded family.

Divorce and remarriage: This might involve someone you don't feel comfortable with.

Relocation: If it's important to you that your children remain in the same school, or location is important to you for some other reason and your first choice for prospective guardian moves away, this may necessitate a change in plans—which means a change in your will.

Health: If your prospective guardian suffers a health crisis that would render him incapable of taking on the responsibility of more children, it's unfair to leave that responsibility hanging over him. Don't forget that substance abuse is one form of health problem.

Drastic change in financial circumstances: If your prospective guardian falls on really hard times, she might not be able to manage the burden of extra children even with your custodial account for them. On the other side of the coin—if she undergoes a striking improvement in financial circumstances, will your kids feel like poor relations?

Drifting apart: It happens in families, or between the best of friends, and there's nothing wrong with acknowledging that in the terms of your will.

Other Stuff About Wills

We tend to think of the distribution of assets when the word *will* is mentioned, and, of course, that is an important part of any will. This is what you should know about your will as a vehicle for distribution of your assets:

If you die without a will, your assets will be divided up according to a preset formula that varies in different states.

You can make bequests in specific amounts, or in terms of a percentage of your total estate. This means you don't have to know exactly how much your estate is worth: You can leave, say, $2,000 to a scholarship fund for your old college and then leave 60 percent of the balance of your estate to your wife, 40 percent to be divided between your children.

You may want to make a contingency plan in your will in case you end up surviving one or more of your beneficiaries. If one of your children dies before you do, you might want your legacy to be divided among your surviving children, but legally the part of the estate left to the child that has died now goes to his estate.

You need to name an executor in your will. The executor will take responsibility for consolidating your assets, paying your bills and taxes, and distributing the balance of your estate to your beneficiaries.

For a simple estate, you may name your spouse or your grown children, or the person you've chosen as guardian for your minor children. For a larger or more complex estate, you may want to hire a professional executor, for a fee. Banks often serve as executors.

Here's what you can't do in a will:

You can't legally disinherit your spouse, but in most states you can legally disinherit your children. If for any reason you should want to disinherit one child but not the others, it's a good idea to specifically mention this in your will, because otherwise the child, if he chooses to challenge the will, can argue that he was inadvertently left out.

You can't leave anyone anything you don't own. This seems

obvious, but it also means you can't leave anyone anything that you don't own outright. If you own an asset jointly—say, a house co-owned with your spouse—you can't will it to someone else. Anything that's legally considered community property—and this varies from state to state—can't be left to anyone else. You can't will the proceeds of insurance policies and pension payments unless you've designated your estate as the beneficiary.

You can't make any bequests that are contrary to sound social policy. For example, if you were to leave money to your daughter on condition that she divorce her husband, it wouldn't hold up in court.

There are other things you can do, but you shouldn't. Simply put: Don't do anything awful with your will. For example, don't put anything in it like "I'm not leaving anything to Cousin Icky because he's a slimeball and a crook," not only because it's unkind, but also because it might be actionable. Libel suits can be filed against an estate.

Even worse, perhaps, is an unfair bequest. Two dear friends of mine, Billie and Jeff, high school teachers in Kentucky, have a blended family—"yours, mine, and ours." They came to the marriage with one child each, and now they have a baby of their own—Philip, aged six months. The older children, Clarice and Beth, are both twelve years old, stepsisters and best friends. Billie had a wealthy aunt who passed away recently, leaving a sizable bequest in trust—for Billie's children only. When Clarice is ready for college, she'll have $300,000, while Beth will be struggling on whatever Billie and Jeff can save. When baby Philip is ready for college, he'll be worth a million dollars.

Billie and Jeff, with rueful humor, have nicknamed Philip "Baby Warbucks," but they don't know what to do. They can't change the terms of the trust. The well-meaning aunt (not entirely well-meaning) has created a terrible inequity in their family.

Drawing Up a Will

You can do this two ways. You can do it yourself, using any of the do-it-yourself will forms that are available from a variety of places (including computer software), or you can have a lawyer do it for you.

The advantage of doing it yourself is that it's inexpensive. If you don't need a lawyer, why pay for one? But this is likely to be an illusory advantage—penny wise and pound foolish. Unless your will is incredibly simple—and it may not be as simple as you think—you might be asking for trouble.

The advantage of using a lawyer is that laws regarding inheritance are complicated, changing from state to state, and not understanding them can lead to serious mistakes that can leave your heirs paying far more in taxes than they need, or keep them tied up in long, expensive court battles, even with their not getting what you wanted them to.

Don't forget—this is your entire estate at stake here; this is everything you've ever worked for, everything you have to pass on. It's not something you want to lose, destroy, or corrupt by nickel-and-diming. I strongly recommend using a lawyer, and I recommend using one who has experience in estate planning.

If you want to save money on will preparation, here's how to do it: Use a lawyer, but go to her office prepared. Lawyers generally charge by the hour, so the more work you've done in advance, the less time you'll spend in the office with the meter running. Here's a checklist of things you'll want to have prepared when you visit your lawyer:

- A complete list of your assets and liabilities. You can use the lists you've already worked out in this book, but you should also consider assets that will continue to work and generate revenue after you're gone, such as rental properties, stocks, and intellectual properties like patents or copyrights.
- A detailed plan of who your beneficiaries are, and how you want to divide your estate among them.

A complete list of specific monetary bequests you want to make. Are there any charities you want to leave money to? Are there friends or distant relatives you want to remember with a small (or even a substantial) bequest before you divide up the rest of your estate?

A complete list of things you own that you want to make specific provision for. Start with large things. Real estate comes first. Your house. A vacation home? Do you own your own business? What's going to happen to all these things? Then go on to your other possessions, such as automobiles, jewelry, antiques, collectibles, collections. Is there someone who would particularly appreciate your record collection, your Hummel figurines, your baseball autographed by the 1969 Mets, your collection of antique wooden carousel horses?

The name(s) of your executor(s) and the guardian(s) for your children. Here's a worksheet to use in preparing for your visit:

Preparing a Will—Cash Items

PERCENTAGE OF CASH ASSETS	BENEFICIARY

(continued on next page)

PERCENTAGE OF CASH ASSETS	BENEFICIARY

Preparing a Will—Items Of Value

ITEM	VALUE	BENEFICIARY
Real Estate		
House		
Vacation home		
Other		
Motor vehicles (identify specifically)		

(continued on next page)

ITEM	VALUE	BENEFICIARY
Jewelry (itemize)		
Silverware/china (itemize)		
Antiques/collectibles/ collections		

Probate

Before your estate can actually be divided among your lega-
tees, it has to go through probate court, which involves a
series of procedures to make sure that your will is valid, that
your assets are properly counted up, and that they are in fact
being divided fairly among your beneficiaries.

The negative things about probate are: The process can take
a long time, it can cost your estate a lot of money, and it is a
public process, which can expose the details of your estate to
anyone who wants to see them.

Some people try to avoid probate altogether. This can be
done in a number of ways, all of which are explained in great
detail in *How to Avoid Probate*, by Norman F. Dacey,
HarperPerennial, $25, but which I'll try to simplify here.

If, as I said above, you can't leave anyone anything that you
don't own outright, then it stands to reason that if you don't
own *anything*, you've got nothing to leave, nothing for a probate court to deal with.

I mentioned before that you can't will the proceeds of insurance policies and pension payments unless you've designated
your estate as the beneficiary. The reverse is equally true: If
you haven't named your estate as the beneficiary, your insurance policy is not part of your will, and is therefore exempt
from probate. This is one way of getting around the probate
court, but it's limited because you can't put all your assets into
insurance.

You can, however, make all of your property jointly owned
"with right of survivorship." Your house may very well already
be jointly owned by you and your spouse; you may have your
money in a joint bank account or a joint brokerage account.
You can put more assets, even all your assets, into joint tenancy with your spouse, your children . . . anyone you want.
This technique is often called the "poor man's will" because it
effectively disposes of your entire estate without any lawyers
or probate courts.

There can be pitfalls, though, in joint tenancy with right of survivorship. Any of them can throw the surviving partner back into probate court.

A joint bank account can be blocked by the bank after the death of one partner, so that the surviving partner is prohibited from drawing on it until a probate process is completed.

Putting all your property, including your bank or brokerage accounts, into joint ownership with another person means that you're always open to the possibility that the other person might clean you out. It's probably not likely, with someone we love and trust enough to share our lives and/or our finances with. We don't like to think about it. But it can happen.

A marriage or a relationship can go bad, and although one partner isn't supposed to be able to empty out an entire bank account, it can happen; and once it's happened, it's very hard to undo.

A beloved child can develop a drug habit, and suddenly be in the grip of a sickness that can deplete financial assets.

A significant other can be involved in a lawsuit. If a judgment is brought against him, it's brought against both of you, and all your assets are at risk.

An unexpected death can wreak havoc with a joint tenancy arrangement. If you own a business, and you put it in joint tenancy with your two children, what happens if one of them dies shortly after you do? You might want his half of the business to go to his heirs, but there may be no provision for that—instead, the whole business will go to the surviving son. Norman F. Dacey also warns against incompetence, citing the case of a husband who registered his securities jointly with his wife, then was unable to dispose of them when she began having periodic bouts of mental illness and was in and out of institutions.

Dacey makes his recommendation in no uncertain terms: "I recommend that you do NOT use joint tenancy."

What Dacey does recommend is a financial strategy called an *inter vivos,* or "living" trust.

Trusts

A trust is a legal entity that is formed to take care of property for someone else. It's sort of like a corporation—in fact, it is like a corporation in that it can own, buy, sell, or transfer assets. What does this mean to you, in terms of avoiding probate and steamlining the transfer of what's yours to those whom you want to transfer it to after you're gone? Well, it means that if these assets don't belong to you directly, if they belong to a trust that's administering them for you, then they're not part of your estate and they don't come under the jurisdiction of a probate court.

This gets around the dilemmas created by a joint tenancy. It also gets around another dilemma.

When you put money in a custodial account for your child, you may budget enough for a college education, but when your child reaches majority, the money belongs to her, and she can spend it in any way she wants. If the money is in trust for her college education, that's what it will go for.

The most popular kind of trust is the revocable inter vivos trust, the living trust, so called because it's a trust you establish when you're still alive.

A trust is created by a *settlor.* He is the person who turns his assets over to the trust. The settlor names a *trustee* whose job it is to take care ot the assets and distribute them to the beneficiaries according to the terms of the trust. In the case of a living trust, the settlor can name himself as trustee, or co-trustee.

❧ Definitions and Data

I've borrowed these concepts—and adapted them freely—from the field of cost accounting—a daunting field if you're not an accountant—but they are worth thinking through. They're good tools, and they can really help you work through your plans for financing your child's life.

Fixed *vs.* Variable Costs

Businesses need to distinguish between *fixed* and *variable costs* in order to determine what are acceptable risks when, for example, they're considering growth. And when you're planning a family, that's exactly what you're considering.

Fixed expenses are the ones you can't tinker with, that you can't fail to meet. Variable costs are ones that may be desirable, but you can do without them if you have to. In a grocery store, for instance, the rental on the building would be a fixed cost; getting in inventory for a new line of products would be a variable cost.

In dealing with the economy of our homes and families, we also deal with the concepts of *need* and *want*. These are very closely related to fixed and variable expenses, but they're not quite the same.

Here's how it works:

Costs are what you have to pay to achieve a specific *cost objective*—a mega-objective, like raising a child from birth until he leaves the house, or a more limited objective, like education.

The *total cost* of education, as an example, is everything that would go on your dream list (see the worksheet at the end of this chapter) under education: a private college, perhaps, plus a private secondary school, plus a Montessori school for preschool and early grades, plus music lessons and computer lessons.

The fixed cost of education is the portion of that total that you have to spend. That can be a very small figure: According to the U.S. Department of Agriculture's Family Economics Research Group, 50 percent of American families spend nothing on it.

Many of us, certainly, will spend a great deal more of that. And for many of us, it's an absolute guarantee that we'll spend more than nothing. That's because a quality education, including higher education, is a need, not a want.

It is in our house. College for my two kids, Kyle and Rhett, is not something we'll spend money on if we have some money left over, which is the definition of a want. It's mandatory. The cost of two college educations is a cost we *have to* budget for.

A private secondary school for us is not a need, not at this time in our lives. I sent Kyle and Rhett to private school when we lived in New York City, and I'm not saying it's impossible that I'd consider it, if it was an extraordinary educational opportunity and we had the extra money. But we live in an area with a great public school system, and I support the concept of public education, so for me, private school is not even on my want list. But when we lived in New York City, it was a high priority want. And certainly some families, for one reason or another, might consider private school a necessity.

College is a need in our family, a mandatory expense. But it's a variable expense. I'd like to send my children to the best private college. But if that much money just isn't available when it's time for them to go, then we'll look at other alternatives, such as our excellent state university system.

This is another important reason why you constantly have to reassess your financial picture, redo your worksheets. What happens if the money simply isn't there? Then some of your needs may have to be redefined as wants; some of your fixed costs may have to be redefined as variable costs.

I send Kyle and Rhett for religious instruction every week, with a wonderful woman, a rabbi's wife. It's an important expense, a very high-priority want, but if we couldn't fit it into the budget, I'd give the kids that religious instruction at home.

Incidentally, an expense can also move from the "want" to the "need" column. If your child's tennis skills may translate into a college scholarship, then you may well decide that tennis lessons are a necessity, not a luxury.

Opportunity Costs

Basically, this means if you buy something now, or commit to buy something now, one of the resources that you're spending is the ability to use that same money to buy something later. One sort of depressing way of way of looking at this: Having a kid means you're incurring an opportunity cost of $334,000 (minimum), which, if you invested it, putting aside the same amount per year that you'll be spending on the kid, would make you a fat cat indeed by the time you were, say, 45 years old.

And some people do make exactly this decision. About seven years ago, I built up a "Financing Your Child's Life" plan for some young friends of mine, Suzanne and Jack, who were thinking about starting a family. When they saw the figures, I could see that they were starting to do some serious thinking. They went into another room to caucus for a few minutes, and when they came back, their minds were made up.

"Forget about it," Suzanne said. "We're not working our

butts off so that twenty-five years from now we can have a couple of kids sitting in a psychiatrist's office telling him what rotten parents we were."

"Absolutely," cracked Jack. "I should spend half a million bucks to get something like me?"

"We'll have nieces and nephews," Suzanne said. "We'll be generous with them."

And they're doing it. They've invested the money they would have spent on having a child. They're generous with their nieces and nephews, they give money to National Public Radio and UNICEF and a variety of other good causes, and they live the life they want. More power to them.

Another way of thinking about it is to weigh the opportunity cost of that new living room furniture in terms of education dollars for college later on.

Return on Investment

There are various measurements that a company can use to figure out how well it's doing, but the one that has come to be considered the most reliable is *rate of return on investment* (ROI), which is the ratio of profit to invested capital. In business, this means the relationship between the amount of money you've invested and the amount of money you're getting back. If it's too low, you've got a problem, and it's an obvious problem: You're not making enough money. If it's too high, you may have a problem, too. Perhaps you're not investing enough capital. You're making a lot of money now, but you're not expanding, you're not putting anything into research and development, and you may be in trouble down the road.

Return on investment is important when you're thinking about your family strategy, too. Take that huge outlay for your kids' college education. It's a major investment . . . what's the return?

Let's look at a couple of different figures here. The first is from the 1993 edition of the *Statistical Abstract of the United States*, published by the U.S. Department of Commerce's census bureau, and it shows a breakdown of how much money people made in relation to how much education they had. (See Table 40 on the next page.)

The second is from *Tomorrow's Jobs*. Bulletin 2400–1 from the U.S. Department of Labor, Bureau of Labor Statistics:

Table 41: Increase of College-Educated People in Work Force, 1993

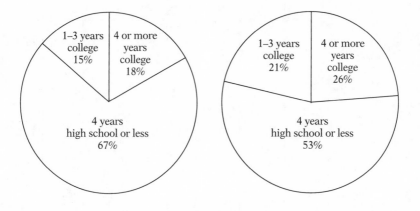

Table 40: Distribution of Income by Education Level

PERCENT DISTRIBUTION OF HOUSEHOLDS BY INCOME LEVEL

LEVEL OF EDUCATION	UNDER $5,000	$5,000–$9,900	$10,000–$14,999	$15,000–$24,999	$25,000–$34,999	$35,000–$49,999	$50,000–$74,999	$75,000 AND OVER	MEDIAN INCOME (DOLLARS)
Less than 9th grade	10.9	26.6	18.2	21.7	10.5	7.4	3.4	1.1	$13,221
9-12 grade, no diploma	9.3	19.7	14.5	22.2	14.0	11.2	6.9	2.2	17,535
High school graduate	4.0	9.5	9.9	19.7	17.8	19.5	14.2	5.5	28,487
Some college, no degree	2.9	6.1	7.7	16.4	16.7	21.5	19.1	9.7	35,150
Associate degree	2.1	4.5	6.0	13.2	16.9	23.0	22.2	12.1	39,700
Bachelor's degree or more	1.3	2.0	3.2	9.1	12.4	19.0	24.9	28.1	52,270
Bachelor's degree	1.3	2.3	3.9	10.7	13.4	20.0	25.8	22.6	48,705
Master's degree	1.4	1.8	2.1	6.8	12.1	19.8	25.2	30.8	55,173
Professional degree	0.9	0.8	2.0	5.6	7.9	11.0	18.2	53.6	77,949
Doctorate degree	0.9	1.3	0.7	4.8	7.9	14.8	22.8	46.9	70,316

The bulletin also says: "Projected rates of employment growth are faster for occupations requiring higher levels of education or training than for those acquiring less.

"The emphasis on education will continue. Three out of the four fastest growing occupational groups will be executive, administrative and managerial; professional specialty; and technicians and related support occupations. These occupations generally require the highest levels of education and skill, and will make up an increasing proportion of new jobs."

A projected rate of return on investment for your child's college education would have to take these figures into account. But remember, when you're talking about your kids and your quality of life, that investment—and profit—will be measured in intangibles as much as in dollars.

Some ROI is simple. If you spend money to give a talented youngster tennis lessons, the potential return on investment— a scholarship—is substantial. But suppose your child doesn't get the scholarship? Is the deal a total loss? It doesn't have to be—not if you remember the value of a sound, athletic body and the feeling of self-worth that can come from taking part and doing one's best. In other words, make sure your child isn't going to feel like a failure if she doesn't get the scholarship, and you have created a different—and important—way of maximizing your return on investment

A good financial planner should be aware of, and able to discuss with you, those intangible quality of life benefits. Do you have *too much* money? That sounds like a problem it would be almost impossible to have, but remember the example above, of the company with too high a profit margin and not enough allocated for research and development. Is your quality of life suffering at the expense of your profits—that is, your savings? Maybe you can afford to remodel the house, and give all of your children their own bedrooms. These are questions you'll have answers to, if you keep track of your intangible as well as your tangible ROI.

Time Value of Money

Sometimes it doesn't only matter how much money you have, or what you allocate it for—it can also make a difference *when* you allocate it. These are the strategies that are covered by the *time value of money* concept, which simply means that your money may be worth more if you spend it now on something you'll need in the future (if prices go up faster than your ability to increase the value of your money by investing). Or it may be worth more if you save it now and buy later (if you can invest it at a better rate than the rate of inflation). Or sometimes it's as simple as this: If you hold on to your money now and keep saving and investing, then when you need to pay for your kids' college there'll be something to pay for it with. In any case, when you sit down with your financial consultant to plan a long-term strategy, time value of money is a concept that should be on both of your minds.

Paying attention to time value of money is an important part of being *proactive*, rather than reactive, and this is an important concept in planning the financing of your child's life. It means, simply, anticipating the decisions you're going to have to make, rather than having them take you by surprise. When it comes to your children, you'll have surprises enough, thank you very much. And when it comes to money, the fewer surprises the better (except maybe winning the lottery, and don't count on that).

According to *Expenditures on a Child by Families: 1993 Technical Report,* compiled by the Family Economics Research Group of the United States Department of Agriculture, the amount that a couple can expect to spend on a child born in 1993, up to age 17, is listed in the table below. The figures are broken into three categories, by family income level.

A *low income* family is defined by FERG as one making less than $32,000—the average income for this group is $20,000. *Middle income* is $32,000 to $54,100—average income $42,600. *High income* is more than $54,100—average income $79,400.

The projected figures assume an average annual inflation rate of 6 percent.

Table 42: Estimated Annual Expenditures on a Child Born in 1993, by Income Group

		FAMILY INCOME BRACKET		
YEAR	AGE	LOW	MIDDLE	HIGH
1993	>1	$ 4,960	$ 6,870	$10,210
1994	1	5,260	7,280	10,820
1995	2	5,570	7,720	11,470
1996	3	6,260	8,600	12,660
1997	4	6,640	9,120	13,420
1998	5	7,040	9,660	14,230
1999	6	7,830	10,580	15,250
2000	7	8,300	11,220	16,160
2001	8	8,800	11,890	17,130
2002	9	8,570	11,790	17,230
2003	10	9,080	12,500	18,270
2004	11	9,620	13,250	19,360
2005	12	11,070	14,870	21,490
2006	13	11,730	15,760	22,780
2007	14	12,430	16,710	24,150

(continued on next page)

		FAMILY INCOME BRACKET		
YEAR	AGE	LOW	MIDDLE	HIGH
2008	15	15,000	19,890	28,260
2009	16	15,900	21,080	29,950
2010	17	16,860	22,350	31,750
TOTAL $		**170,920**	**231,140**	**334,590**

As the compilers of the survey point out, it is somewhat unrealistic to assume that households remain in one income category as a child grows older. For most families, income rises over time. In addition, such projections assume child-rearing expenditures change only with inflation, when in fact parental expenditure patterns tend to change over time.

Sue and Dan are in the high-income bracket—they're hard workers, and they have a reasonable expectation that they're going to go on working, and advancing in their chosen fields. So they are going to have to budget close to a minimum of $700,000 over the next twenty years for their two children. That's FERG's $334,590 times two—they're rounding it up because inflation will inflate the figure for the second child, and besides, they have a feeling the real numbers will be a lot higher.

The previous table showed how much an average American family will spend on *one child*—an infant born in 1993—over the next seventeen years. This table breaks the spending down into categories and shows how much the average American family spent in *one year*—1993—on children of different age levels.

Table 43: Estimated Annual Expenditures on a Child by Husband-Wife Families, 1993

Age	Total	Housing	Food	Trans- portation	Clothing	Health/ Education	Child Care	Other
Low income (Less than $32,000; average: $20,000)								
0–2	$4,000	$1,870	$730	$720	$380	$330	$530	$400
3–5	5,260	1,910	830	740	380	330	600	470
6–8	5,520	1,830	1,040	960	450	370	290	580
9–11	5,070	1,490	1,240	810	450	410	180	490
12–14	5,500	1,530	1,220	1,010	720	380	110	530
15–17	5,260	1,550	1,490	1,270	730	460	220	540
Total	97,710	30,540	19,650	16,530	9,330	6,840	5,790	9,030
Middle income ($32,000 to $54,100; average: $42,600)								
0–2	6,870	2,560	870	1,080	450	410	840	660
3–5	7,200	2,600	1,020	1,100	440	400	930	730
6–8	7,460	2,520	1,270	1,320	530	470	510	840
9–11	6,980	2,190	1,500	1,170	520	510	340	750
12–14	7,390	2,220	1,490	1,370	830	470	220	790
15–17	8,300	2,250	1,750	1,650	850	560	440	800
Total	132,660	43,020	23,700	23,070	10,860	8,460	9,840	13,710
High income (more than $54,100; average: $79,400)								
0–2	10,210	4,050	1,200	1,330	600	480	1,320	1,230
3–5	10,630	4,090	1,370	1,360	600	480	1,430	1,300
6–8	10,750	4,010	1,620	1,580	700	560	870	1,410
9–11	10,200	3,670	1,870	1,430	690	600	620	1,320

(continued on next page)

Age	Total	Housing	Food	Trans-portation	Clothing	Health/Education	Child Care	Other
High Income (more than $54,100; average: $79,400)								
12–14	10,680	3,710	1,890	1,630	1,090	570	430	1,360
15–17	11,790	3,730	2,140	1,920	1,110	660	860	1,370
Total	192,780	69,780	30,270	27,750	14,370	10,050	16,590	23,710

The figures in all of these tables come from the 1990 Consumer Expenditure Survey (CE), updated to 1993 dollars. The survey was administered by the Bureau of Labor Statistics and represents the most comprehensive source of household expenditure information available at the national level.

It is accurate—and it is also low. I mean, really low. That is to say, don't count on actually spending these amounts yourself on your own children; it's very likely you'll spend more. For example, the Child Care and Education figure represents the national average. But included in that average figure is approximately 50 percent of the population, which spent no money at all in this category—they didn't send their kids to day-care of any sort, never hired a baby-sitter, sent their kids to public schools and didn't spend anything on books or supplies, didn't give their kids any special lessons or enrichment programs. So these figures are an odd anomaly. They're real . . . but they're not realistic.

Sue and Dan, looking at this table, realized that they were likely to have to estimate their own expenses even higher. "I know we're going to be spending a lot more than that on education," Sue said.

"Right," said Dan. "I hope we'll be able to send the kids to a good public school, but even so—there are books, reference books, educational software . . . "

"Summer camp," said Sue. "Special classes in things they're interested in . . . "

"Well, we know one thing," said Dan. "We'll have to make up our own budget."

Here is a breakdown of all the expenses that are actually covered in this survey:

Housing expenses: shelter (mortgage interest, property taxes, or rent; maintenance and repairs; insurance), utilities (gas, electricity, fuel, telephone, water), and house furnishings and equipment (furniture, floor coverings, major appliances, small appliances). It should be noted that for homeowners, housing expenses do not include mortgage principal payments; such payments are considered in the CE to be a part of savings. Hence, total dollars allocated to housing by homeowners are underestimated in this report.

Food expenditures: food and nonalcoholic beverages purchased at grocery stores, convenience stores, and specialty stores; dining out at restaurants; and school meals.

Transportation expenses: the net outlay on the purchase of new and used vehicles, vehicle finance charges, gasoline and motor oil, maintenance and repairs, insurance, and public transportation.

Clothing expenses: children's apparel items such as diapers, shirts, pants, dresses, and suits; footwear; and clothing services such as dry cleaning, alteration and repair, and storage.

Health care expenses: medical and dental services not covered by insurance, prescription drugs and medical supplies not covered by insurance, and health insurance premiums not paid by employer or other organization.

Child care and education expenses: day-care tuition and supplies; baby-sitting; and elementary and high school tuition, books and supplies.

Other miscellaneous expenses: personal care items, entertainment, and reading materials.

"This means," said Sue, "that they're not talking about all the money people spend while their children are growing up, just all the money they spend that they wouldn't have spent if they hadn't had children."

For a single-parent family, here are the comparable figures for a single year (calculated for 1993):

Table 44: Estimated Annual Expenditures on a Child by Single-Parent Families, 1993

AGE OF CHILD	FAMILY INCOME	
	LESS THAN $32,000 (AVERAGE: $13,700)	$32,000 OR MORE (AVERAGE: $47,900)
0–2	$4,310	$9,600
3–5	4,970	10,370
6–8	5,710	11,320
9–11	4,980	10,310
12–14	5,350	10,860
15–17	6,400	11,850

Single-parent expenditures tend to be lower in general, because single parents have less money. While a third of husband-wife families fall in the low-income category, 84 percent of single-parent families fall in this category, and the average income within the category is a lot lower.

Single-parent families, in this lower income group, spend a larger proportion of their income on children. On average, housing and clothing expenses were higher for this group; transportation, health care, child care and education, and miscellaneous goods and services were lower; food expenditures were about the same.

Table 45: Adjustments for Household Size

ONE-CHILD HOUSEHOLD		
AGE OF CHILD		**ANNUAL EXPENDITURE**
0–2		$8,660 = (6,870 x 1.26)
3–5		9,100 = (7,220 x 1.26)
6–8		9,400 = (7,460 x 1.26)
9–11		8,790 = (6,980 x 1.26)
12–14		9,310 = (7,390 x 1.26)
15–17		10,460 = (8,300 x 1.26)

TWO-CHILD HOUSEHOLD		
AGE OF YOUNGER CHILD	**AGE OF OLDER CHILD**	**ANNUAL EXPENDITURE**
0–2	16	$15,170 = (6,870 + 8,300)
3–5	16	15,520 = (7,220 + 8,300)
6–8	16	15,760 = (7,460 + 8,300)
9–11	16	15,280 = (6,980 + 8,300)
12–14	16	15,690 = (7,390 + 8,300)
15	16	16,600 = (8,300 + 8,300)

(continued on next page)

THREE-CHILD HOUSEHOLD

AGE OF YOUNGER CHILD	AGE OF OLDER CHILD	ANNUAL EXPENDITURE
0–2	13, 16	$17,600 = [(6,870 + 7,390 + 8,300) x 0.78]
3–5	13, 16	17,870 = [(7,220 + 7,390 + 8,300) x 0.78]
6–8	13, 16	18,060 = [(7,460 + 7,390 + 8,300) x 0.78]
9–11	13, 16	17,680 = [(6,980 + 7,390 + 8,300) x 0.78]
12	13, 16	18,000 = [(7,390 + 7,390 + 8,300) x 0.78]

The figures estimated in the tables above represent the expenditures for one child in a two-child family.

For a two-parent family, expenses for a second child are approximately the same. Expenses for an only child are approximately 126 percent of the amount for one child in a two-child family. Expenses for three or more children are approximately 78 percent of the amount.

In the case of a single parent family with two children, the expense on the second child is approximately 92 percent of the amount for the first one. Expenses for an only child are approximately 137 percent of the amount for one child in a two-child family. Expenses for three or more children are approximately 72 percent of the amount.

FERG's table shows the estimated annual expenditures for sample households with one, two, and three children in 1993. The calculations are for households in the middle-income group. The figures in the annual expenditure column work like this:

The first figure ($8,660 in the first entry) represents the total of what an average family spends in a year on all its children. The first figure inside the parentheses is the base figure for the younger child in a two-parent family, the one we've been working with in the earlier tables. The rest of it is the calculation you have to do to arrive at the total. For an only child, you multiply by 126 percent. For two kids, you just add the two figures together—in the example, the last figure is always the same because they're assuming 16 years old, in every case, as the age of the older child. For three kids, you add the three figures together and multiply by 78 percent.

A friend showed these tables to Sue and Dan. "It says here you'll be spending another half a million dollars on your kids by the time they get to be seventeen years old," she told them

"Sounds like a lot of money," Dan said.

"On the other hand, it said you've already spent about $150,000."

"Well, if we managed that, we can manage the rest. We'll just have to plan it out."